HOW TO BUY

GOVERNMENT FORECLOSURES

VOLUME I

YOUR *COMPLETE* GUIDE
TO BUYING DISCOUNT HOMES!

By
Rebecca A. Harris
And
Thomas J. Stewart

Clarendon House Inc, Publishers

Library of Congress Catalog Card Number: TX4-145-255

ISBN 1-886908-00-1
2nd Edition

Printed in the United States of America

Acknowledgments

We would like to thank the hard-working representatives of the state and federal government agencies we talked to in the course of writing this book—the FDIC, HUD, SBA, IRS, VA, GSA, Fannie Mae/Freddie Mac, and more! Also, a big thank you to the folks in local government offices as well. We spent many hours on the telephone with these individuals, and found them extremely helpful and willing to provide the up-to-date information included here—information that will make it easier for you to find foreclosed properties. Their assistance is what made this book possible!

A Note from the Publisher

We have made every effort to ensure the accuracy of the information we report. However, we cannot be held responsible for any errors that may have inadvertently been made, or for changes in any of the information since we went to print.

Also, please note that we are not affiliated with any of the government agencies or real estate business entities referred to in this book. Neither are we able to offer legal, technical, accounting, or financial advice. We urge the reader to always consult with his or her professional advisor before proceeding.

Table of Contents

Foreword

We're delighted that you chose to buy this book! We think you'll find *How to Buy Government Foreclosures* is one of the most complete books of its kind on the market today.

The information contained within these pages is a real gold mine of opportunity—just waiting for you to go prospecting! Our researchers have discovered the latest developments at the government agencies that sell fore-closed properties. Now we're able to pass that valuable information on to you, to make it easier for you to find INCREDIBLE homes at UNBELIEV-ABLE prices!

There are over a dozen Federal and State government agencies to choose from, and countless special programs at the local level for first-time home buyers and people with low to moderate incomes—you'll be truly amazed by the options presented here! With all the bargain homes on the market, there's no reason why one of them shouldn't belong to you!

Which brings us to one last word of advice: homes aren't bought over-night! While this book can make your job easier, it DOES take some persis-tence and determination on your part to become a homeowner. Don't make just one or two phone calls and then give up. These government agencies exist to help people just like you buy their dream homes—all you have to do is meet them halfway.

Use this book as your guide, coach, and cheering squad, and you'll be sure to find the home you want, at the price you can afford. Happy house hunting!

—The Publisher

Introduction

Welcome to the world of foreclosures and bargain real estate! There REALLY IS a wonderful world of bargain homes out there, <u>just waiting for you!</u> We know this is true because we've seen it in person—through the hundreds of hours we've spent gathering the information contained in this book!

Foreclosure is a nationwide phenomenon—and one that is still on the rise. In California alone, foreclosures went up 19% in the first eight months of 1994—and that's on top of a 70% increase in foreclosures between 1992 and 1993! While some areas of the country may see more foreclosures than others, you'll find HUNDREDS of deals in real estate foreclosures wherever you go. <u>The trick is knowing how to find them—and that's where this book comes in!</u>

Within these pages you, the prospective home buyer, will find helpful information on a dozen Federal and State government agencies, plus other local and regional sources of foreclosure properties. You'll learn how to contact these agencies about the foreclosures they have for sale. You'll find insider's tips that give you a leading edge when it comes to placing offers on these properties.

You'll also learn about sources for home mortgages with LOW down payments—as little as 5% down!—and the LOWEST interest rates around! <u>There are many government programs designed especially for low to moderate income home buyers</u>—programs whose sole purpose is to help YOU buy the home of your dreams. We tell you all about these programs in this book—then you can choose the one that's best for you!

In the course of our research, we've seen list after list of foreclosure properties. Just like people, these properties come in all shapes and sizes. They range from humble frame houses to magnificent mansions—from single-family dwellings to duplexes, triplexes, and fourplexes—and from raw land to commercial real estate. <u>And most of these properties are available at prices you'll have to see to believe!</u>

We know that after you read this volume, you'll want to get ahold of lists of foreclosure properties RIGHT AWAY! With that in mind, we have created **Volume 2** of *How to Buy Government Foreclosures*—which brings you up-to-the-minute lists of foreclosure properties available from many of the agencies referred to in this book! We've made Volume 2 complimentary with the purchase of Volume 1—and we think you'll find there's no easier way to take advantage of these great deals!

Despite the changes the 1990s have brought to the American economy and workplace, home ownership is still the great American dream—and it's still a dream that can come true for <u>YOU</u>! This book has all the information you need to get the ball rolling—now it's up to you to use it! If you take the time to explore the many options presented here, you'll be richly rewarded when you walk through the front door of your new dwelling—<u>knowing that you paid a bargain price for the home of YOUR dreams!</u>

Chapter 1:
Overview and Fast Start

This book is designed to give you a fast and easy start down the road to finding foreclosed properties. Below you'll see a brief summary of the chapters in this book and their contents. Use this as a checklist as you go along, and you'll leave no stone unturned in your search for IN-CREDIBLE DEALS on real estate foreclosures!

We begin with a review of your finances. **Chapter 2, Your Finances,** takes you step by step through a personal financial review. You'll learn the four keys to financial readiness, why there will never be a better time to buy than right now, the tax benefits of home ownership, and how to repair your credit.

Then we move on to budgeting and evaluating your borrowing power. This chapter includes worksheets to help you discover your total assets, total liabilities, how much you can afford for your monthly mortgage payment, and how much you can afford to pay for a house!

Chapter 3, Loan Sources, makes mortgages simple! First we talk about the most common types of lenders and how to find good lenders. Then we go over the types of mortgages, one by one—including conventional mortgages (30, 25, 20, and 15 year, complete with cost comparisons!); bi-weekly mortgages, balloon mortgages, wraparound mortgages, two-step mortgages, adjustable rate mortgages (ARMs), and buydown mortgages.

Also in Chapter 3, you'll learn about FHA loans, VA loans, private mortgage insurance (PMI), assumptions—and even some ideas for good old mom and dad mortgages! Then, we show you some creative ways to cut your down payment down to size. At the end of the chapter, you'll find a Loan Profile Chart that you can copy and use to record information about different types of loans as you proceed with your search.

Chapter 4, Your Strategy, guides you through the process of finding the bargain home that's right for YOU. We talk about what makes the perfect bargain home, your key to success with bargain homes, and four questions to ask yourself before buying a home. Then we show you how to find good neighborhoods and real estate professionals to assist you in your search. You'll find other sections on the importance of LOCATION, how to price the home you want, how to place an offer, how to reduce closing costs, and how to buy at auction.

Chapter 5, HUD Programs, gives you the lowdown on some great programs for low to middle income home buyers. These programs have been recently revamped, and you'll find the latest information here about how to take advantage of HUD bargains!

Chapter 6, Bank Foreclosures and REOs, gives you some basic definitions and information about the ins and outs. We show you five ways to find these amazing deals and tell you what to watch out for in the process. Then we go into the rules of foreclosure auctions and REO sales. A sample offer letter to a bank for an REO property is included for your use. Finally, you get the complete rundown on bankruptcy sales—another potential gold mine for you!

Chapter 7, Delinquent Tax Sales, describes another area of great opportunities for discount homes: properties with unpaid federal, state, or property taxes that are sold at public auction. You'll read about the fast track to bargains, what to watch out for when you visit the property, investigating liens, how to set your bid, and what to do at the auction.

Chapter 8, Probate and Estate Sales, explores this little-known area of finding real estate bargains. You'll learn how to find these properties, why it's important not to judge a book by its cover, what happens during a probate or estate sale, and how to swing a private sale before the auction date.

Chapter 9, IRS Sales, takes a look at the great deals available on properties seized by the IRS for nonpayment of taxes. You'll find out about the risks and the rewards, as well as the importance of a title search, the six-month redemption period, where to find these sales, and a list of IRS regional offices.

Chapter 10, GSA Sales, reveals the secrets of buying surplus Federal property from the GSA, or General Services Administration. This agency has a long history of offering incredible bargains, and this chapter shows you exactly where to go and what to do to find them! A list of GSA regional and field offices is included.

Chapter 11, VA Repossessions, is not just for veterans—ANYONE can buy a repo from the Veterans Administration or assume a VA loan! This chapter explains how to find VA repos and how to place a bid, with insider's tips to guide you to the best deals.

Chapter 12, FDIC Sales, explains how the Federal Deposit Insurance Corporation resells foreclosed properties from failed banks. A special benefit is the FDIC's Affordable Housing Program, which reserves certain properties for purchase by families with low to moderate incomes. You'll find out how to get the scoop on FDIC houses and how to make an offer. A list of FDIC regional offices and a sample property list are included.

Chapter 13, State Surplus Sales, describes how State governments occasionally sell properties that used to belong to State agencies. This is a great and little-known source of bargain real estate, and some of these properties even have historic value! This chapter will show you how to track them down, complete with a list of State Surplus agencies.

Chapter 14, Rural Properties and Farmland, shows you the way to Green Acres and the rural lifestyle! Big changes are afoot: the long-standing Farmer's Home Administration agency has been replaced with two new agencies. Rural Economic and Community Development now handles rural home loans, and the Consolidated Farm Service Agency handles farm loans. You'll get all the details in this information-packed chapter!

Chapter 15, Fannie Mae and Freddie Mac, provides a clear explanation of what these Federal loan agencies do, and don't do, for you. You'll discover Fannie Mae's Community Home Buyers Program, for low-cost loans to low and moderate income folks; and Freddie Mac's Affordable Gold Loans, NeighborWorks Loans, and HomeWorks loans. Lists of Fannie Mae and Freddie Mac offices are included.

Chapter 16, Small Business Administration (SBA) Sales, tells you all about the SBA's National Office of Liquidation, which oversees the sale of foreclosed properties. This is another great and little-known source of real estate bargains, just waiting for the taking by savvy buyers like you! A list of SBA Field Offices is included.

Chapter 17, Home Inspection, guides you through the process of inspecting your foreclosure or bargain home BEFORE you buy. You'll learn what to look for, the warning signs of potential problems, and when you should hire a professional inspector to do the job. The chapter features complete checklists for your own home inspection!

About The Back of the Book

At the end of this book, you'll find additional information in the Appendices to aid you in your search. The Glossary defines most of the real estate and financial terms used throughout the book, and the Bibliography gives you plenty of sources for further reading on buying foreclosures and bargain homes.

So there you have it! Now you know why we call this your COMPLETE guide to buying discount homes! With this information in hand, you have everything you need to start your search TODAY—so get ready, and we'll see you in Chapter 2!

P.S. DON'T FORGET that the book you're now holding is *How to Buy Government Foreclosures, Volume 1*—wait til you hear about Volume 2! Volume 2 brings you the latest listings of ACTUAL PROPERTIES from the agencies we talk about here—it's the perfect companion to Volume 1!

Chapter 2:
Your Finances

A home is likely to be the biggest purchase you make in a life-time. It also has the potential to be the best investment you ever made—and it's the ONLY investment you can actually live in!

That said, exactly how much money will you need to move in? The answer is—while the exact amount varies wildly, it's probably less than you think! <u>The housing market abounds with properties that owners are willing to sell at almost any cost.</u> With persistence, you can find and own the home of your dreams!

This chapter will help you organize your personal finances to set the stage for success. When you go to a Realtor, mortgage loan officer, or banker for professional advice, <u>you'll be far ahead of the game if you've read this chapter.</u>

Look around you at all the people who own homes. They all lived through the financial challenges to get there—*and you can, too!* Always re-member that bankers are in business to give home loans to people just like you. They have a vested interest in working with you to get your loan ap-proved. Here's what you can do to meet them halfway.

The Four Keys to Financial Readiness

When you go to apply for a loan, most lenders evaluate the following four factors to determine your financial readiness for home ownership:

1. A consistent record of paying bills on time.
Do you pay your monthly bills on time? This means your phone bill, gas and electric bills, rent, and any other fixed monthly payments. Most lenders want to see a two-year record of on-time monthly payments. If you have

overdue bills, now's the time to bring them up to date. A squeaky-clean payment record will make you very attractive to potential lenders. See the section on credit later in this chapter for more details.

2. A record of steady employment.

Exactly what does this mean? Lenders typically want to see two years of work for the same employer—or, if you've worked for more than one employer, evidence of progress in your chosen field. There are many exceptions to this rule, however. In some lines of work, such as sales, frequent job changes are normal. Exceptions can also be made if you've just finished school, job training, or military service; if your work is typically seasonal; or if you've been laid off in the past two years because of downsizing or illness.

3. An acceptable level of debt vs. income.

Lenders will take a close look at your debt-to-income ratio when determining your ability to repay a loan. There are two rules of thumb: lenders prefer that your mortgage payment, home insurance, and property taxes not exceed 28% of your gross monthly income. Also, the total of your mortgage payment plus all your other long-term debts—things like car loans, credit card payments, school tuition, and major appliances—should not exceed 36% of your gross monthly income.

4. Savings to cover the home's down payment and closing costs.

Do you have enough money in the bank to cover these important items? If not, it might be too early to apply for a home loan. You'll benefit by taking the time to put more money in the bank before sitting down with your lender. This is not an insurmountable task. In today's economic climate, most lenders are willing to settle for a 5% to 10% down payment. And don't forget—there are MANY creative ways to come up with the money—we'll be talking about some of them in the next chapter.

WHY Are Today's Homes So Expensive?

It's easy to get discouraged about the high prices of homes these days. Back in the 1970s, first-time buyers all over the country could easily find an average starter house for under $40,000. Today that same house can be worth over $140,000.

Real estate values soared during the 1980s—which was GREAT for homeowners, but NOT SO GREAT for buyers looking to enter the market. In the 1990s, it's unlikely that we'll see such dramatic increases in selling prices—but it's a sure bet that housing prices will continue to rise, at least at the same rate as the cost of living. Prices can be expected to decline in areas of the country that are affected by economic downturns, and to rise at slightly faster rates in urban centers where local economies are expanding.

What does all this mean to you, the prospective buyer? <u>No matter what part of the country you live in, there will probably never be a better time than now to buy!</u> About the only reasons to delay buying a home are: if you anticipate a job transfer in the near future, or if you need time to get your finances in order. Also, if the local economy is on the fritz, you may want to wait til the upswing to protect your investment. Every buying situation needs to be evaluated carefully to make sure your prospective home is a diamond in the rough, not a lemon that will turn your investment sour.

P.S. Don't Forget the Tax Benefits of Home Ownership!

You're probably familiar with tax write-offs for mortgage interest. That's one of the big perks of home ownership, and one of the benefits you'll enjoy when you move up from renting to buying a home.

<u>The good news is that home ownership may lead to other deductions, some of which are not even related to housing!</u> As a homeowner, you must use Form 1040, which allows you to itemize deductions. You can write off not only mortgage interest, but also property taxes, state income taxes, and charitable contributions. *In special cases, you may also be able to write off medical bills, theft losses, moving expenses, and other miscellaneous items.*

There are other long-term tax benefits. <u>When you sell your home and buy another of equal or greater value, you can defer the tax on any profit from the sale.</u> Interest on money borrowed for home improvements is deductible. *You can even use your home as security to borrow money for major purchases like a new car, and then write off the interest!*

Finally, when you reach age 55, you can take advantage of a one-time opportunity to sell your home and shield up to $125,000 in profits from federal taxes. Now THAT'S something renters won't have to look forward to—and all the more reason to consider buying as soon as you're able!

What If Your Credit is "Bad"?

So many of us have less-than-perfect credit ratings. If you have "bad credit," you're not alone—and you know it's not just a matter of being irresponsible about your bills. We can all experience tough financial situations that set us back for awhile—whether it's a period of unemployment, a messy divorce, or a serious illness.

The question is, what do you do when your bad credit rating hangs around long after the crisis is over? The reporting period for negative information on your credit record is seven years—10 years in the case of bankruptcy. Poor credit can be an obstacle to many things, from getting a major credit card to buying a home.

The first step in dealing with your credit situation is to request a copy of your credit report. Unless you have it, you won't know how much it reveals about your past financial problems. The Fair Credit Reporting Act (FCRA) guarantees you the right to review your credit report and correct any misinformation, if necessary. Remember that credit bureaus have been known to make mistakes, too. It's not surprising, given that there are nearly 1,000 credit bureaus operating in the U.S.!

Every credit bureau gets their data from one of three information agencies: TRW, Trans Union, or Equifax. You can request a copy of your credit report by calling them at the numbers listed below:

TRW: (800) 682-7654
Trans Union: (312) 408-1050
Equifax: (800) 685-1111

When you call, you will be asked to provide proper identification and to make your request in writing. It usually takes about 30 days to receive your report in the mail. If you request a credit report in writing within 30 days of being denied credit, the FCRA states that the report must be provided free of charge. Otherwise, the fee will range from $2 to $20.

If you find that your credit report lists errors—for example, accounts that you have paid are still listed as unpaid—it's up to you to set the record straight! Supply the facts to the credit agency in writing. Be sure you have the proof to back up your claim—the agency won't investigate or drop outdated information from your report if they think your claim is "frivolous."

A final note: AVOID the credit repair clinics you see advertised in the backs of magazines or the classified sections of newspapers! Most of them charge you *hundreds of dollars* for advice that will probably do NOTHING to improve your credit rating!

CREDIT SUCCESS TIP

Improve your credit rating NOW by adding new, positive references to your credit report. For example, a bankcard—Visa, MasterCard, or Discover—paid on time, over time, is one of the best credit references you can have—EVEN BETTER than a mortgage!

Regardless of your past credit, you can usually obtain a secured credit card from a bank. This is a credit card backed by a deposit equal to your credit limit. You agree to keep the deposit in the bank for as long as you have the card.

After you establish a track record of payments, you'll be able to obtain a regular, unsecured credit card—and you'll be well on your way to establishing great credit!

Focus on Your Financial Picture

The time to clarify your financial picture is NOW, before you even find the home of your dreams! Use the charts on the next two pages to make a complete inventory of your financial assets and liabilities.

Your <u>ASSETS</u> include everything that you own that has cash value. Use the financial assets chart to put a dollar amount after each item, entering the value at which the item could be sold for today. Add these amounts and place the total at the bottom of the chart.

Your <u>LIABILITIES</u> are your debts. Use the financial liabilities chart to list all your debts and the amounts owed for each. The total will be the money you need to completely pay off your debts. Do not count regular monthly expenses like food and utilities.

After you've filled in the charts, subtract your total liabilities from your total assets to get your <u>FINANCIAL NET WORTH</u>. Now you know where you stand! You can use this information to set financial goals for next year, five years from now, and ten years from now. By taking charge of your finances in this way, home ownership can definitely be yours.

My Financial Assets

Cash

800.   ___ Cash on hand
200. 100. ___ Savings accounts
            ___ Checking accounts
       —   ___ Money market funds

Liquid investments

       —   ___ Stocks
       —   ___ Savings Bonds
       —   ___ Mutual funds
     800.   ___ Life insurance policies (cash value)
            ___ Other

       —   _ Long-term CDs
       —   _ IRAs
       —   _ Keoghs
       ?   _ Employee retirement/savings plan
       —   _ Long-term loans to others
            _ Other

Property

14000, 4,000   Cars
3000, 3500,   Recreational vehicles and equipment
  7500,   Household furnishings
    1800   Tools
   3 600   Clothing, Furs, Jewelry
                Art and Antiques
    1000   Collections
                Rental property
                Other real estate or personal assets

            _ TOTAL FINANCIAL ASSETS

My Financial Liabilities

Loans

_____ Car, boat, and camper loans

_____ Furniture and appliance loans

_____ Education loans

_____ Vacation loans

_____ Other installment loans

_____ Other

Unpaid bills

_____ Taxes

_____ Charge accounts

_____ Credit card balances

_____ Past due alimony/child support

_____ Doctor and dentist bills

_____ Other

Mortgages

_____ Home, rental property,

_____ and other mortgage loans

_____ TOTAL FINANCIAL LIABILITIES

The "B" Word: Budgeting

Does money burn a hole in your pocket? Many people have no idea where their money goes. *The truth is, you may have more money than you think!* Try this: write down everything you spend money on, down to the smallest pocket change items, every day for one month. This can be a real eye opener.

Miracles can truly happen when you take charge of your spending. A monthly budget helps you set priorities and save money for the items you

REALLY want—like a home of your own! <u>Even if you thought you could never save, get into the habit of paying yourself first every month.</u> Think of it as a fixed expense, like any other monthly bill. You can even have your bank transfer a set amount from your checking account to your savings account on a monthly basis!

By establishing good savings habits, you'll prove to the bank—and yourself—that you can actually afford to buy the home you want. Because you're going to have to lay out some money up front for . . .

The Down Payment

In the current housing market, down payments are the downfall of homebuyers—especially first-time homebuyers. With prices higher than ever before, the traditional 20% down payment is going the way of the dinosaur. Lenders recognize that most people just don't have that kind of money.

<u>Instead, most lenders are willing to deal if you can offer between 5% and 10% of the purchase price in cash.</u> If you need to supplement your savings with money from other sources to get your down payment, consult Chapter 3 for creative solutions and various loan options—*for example, FHA loans which allow a 5% down payment—or VA loans which require no down payment at all!*

Rule of Thumb for Down Payments:

The BIGGER your down payment, the BETTER terms you'll get on your mortgage—including LOWER monthly payments and LOWER interest rates!

What's Your Borrowing Power?

If you have enough money to pay cash for the home you want, chances are you're not reading this book. Most would-be homeowners expect to take on a mortgage. *The question is, how big a mortgage can you qualify for?*

The answer to this question begins with PITI. PITI stands for the four components of your monthly mortgage payment: principal, interest, taxes, and insurance. Fill in the blanks and use the chart on the following pages to figure the PITI payment you can afford.

Ready, Set, Go!

Once you've filled out the forms at the end of this chapter, and used the Mortgage Payment Calculator Chart to figure out your monthly payment, you're ready to move on to Chapter 3—Loan Sources. There, you'll find out how to use your hard-earned dollars to the best advantage in the housing market. You won't BELIEVE how many options there are for loans with very little money down, and very attractive monthly payments.

If you've made it this far, *congratulations*—you've got what it takes to find and own a bargain home. Now it's only a matter of time before you reach your goal—and that could be MUCH sooner than you think!

PITI Payment Worksheet

1. What is your total monthly income? (Gross salaries, bonuses, average commissions, alimony and child support, interest and dividend income, etc.)

2. Multiply your monthly income by .36 and enter the amount here:
(The maximum amount of debt most lenders will allow is 36% of your monthly income.)

3. What is your total monthly debt? (Car payments, credit card minimum payments, alimony, child support, and other obligations. Exclude your current rent or mortgage payment, food, clothing, and utilities.)

4. Subtract Line 3 from Line 2.
This is the amount you can afford for PITI—your monthly mortgage payment

How Much House Can You Afford?

Use the following worksheet to figure exactly how much you can afford to pay for a house.

1. Enter the amount you can afford for PITI here:
(See Line 4 from the previous worksheet)

_____

2. Multiply the amount on Line 1 by .16
(On average, 16% of the PITI payment is held in escrow for property taxes and insurance.)

_____

3. Subtract Line 2 from Line 1.
(This amount equals the principal and interest portion of your monthly payment.)

_____

4. Consult the Mortgage Payment Calculator Table on the next page. Look under the column closest to the current interest rate, finding the closest figure to

the amount you entered on Line 3 above. Then scan to
the left to see how big a mortgage you can afford. Enter
the mortgage amount here. _____

5. Enter the amount you can comfortably afford for a down
payment: _____

6. Add Lines 4 and 5. The total equals what you can afford
to pay for a house. _____

Mortgage Payment Calculator Chart

Monthly principal and interest payments on a 30-year, fixed-rate mortgage.
Escrow payments for property taxes and insurance are not included.

Mtg. amt.	8.0%	8.125%	8.25%	8.375%	8.5%	8.675%	8.75%	8.875%
$50,000	$366.88	371.07	375.63	380.03	384.45	390.49	393.35	397.64
$60,000	$440.25	445.28	450.75	456.04	461.34	468.59	472.02	477.17
$70,000	$513.63	519.50	525.88	531.80	538.23	546.69	550.69	556.70
$80,000	$587.01	593.71	601.01	607.77	615.13	624.79	629.36	636.22
$90,000	$660.38	667.93	676.13	683.74	692.02	702.89	708.03	715.75
$100,000	$733.76	742.14	751.26	759.71	768.91	780.99	786.70	795.28
$110,000	$807.14	816.36	826.39	835.69	845.80	859.09	865.37	874.81
$120,000	$880.51	890.57	901.51	911.66	922.69	937.19	944.04	954.34
$130,000	$953.89	964.79	976.64	987.63	999.58	1015.29	1022.71	1033.87
$140,000	$1027.27	1039.00	1051.77	1063.60	1076.47	1093.39	1101.38	1113.40
$150,000	$1100.64	1113.22	1126.89	1139.57	1153.37	1171.49	1180.05	1192.92
$160,000	$1174.02	1187.43	1202.02	1215.55	1230.26	1249.58	1258.72	1272.45

Chapter 3:
Loan Sources

Lenders, lenders everywhere—there's no shortage of lenders when it comes to home financing. Lenders are all alike in one respect: their business is to make money by loaning YOU money—and they'll be more than happy to provide the money for your mortgage as long as they can make a profit on the deal!

<u>What you must keep in mind is that lenders are as different from each other as they are alike.</u> Lender A may make you jump through hoops, while Lender B may give you a loan practically on the spot. Lender A may make you feel like you'll never get a loan, while Lender B will bend over backwards and make it happen!

<u>The point is, you must take advantage of the differences between lenders to get yourself the best mortgage.</u> The way to do this is to **TAKE YOUR TIME and SHOP AROUND.** There are MANY types of lenders who make home loans. In your search for a mortgage, you'll get acquainted with at least some of the following:

- Mortgage companies
- National and state commercial banks
- Federal and state savings banks
- Federal and state savings and loans
- Mutual savings banks
- Industrial banks
- Insurance companies
- Credit unions
- Finance companies
- Credit corporations
- Mortgage brokers

How To Find Good Lenders

The best place to start is by word of mouth. ASK PEOPLE YOU KNOW who've bought homes where they got their mortgages. Get names and phone numbers of their lenders, then CALL those lenders and tell them who sent you. If lenders know that you're a referral customer, you should get extra special treatment!

The next place to look is your local newspaper. Get in the habit of reading the real estate section regularly. You'll see advertisements by lenders who specialize in low interest mortgages, like the examples on the next page. **Call these folks and let them strut their stuff for you!**

Finally, you can look in the yellow pages of your phone book under the following headings: Banks, Real Estate Loans, Mortgages, and Mortgage Loans. <u>Call as many of the lenders listed as you can!</u> It's impossible to call too many of them—the lender with the best deal may be just the next phone call away!

We know a fellow who proved the success of this approach by calling <u>EVERY SINGLE LENDER</u> he could find in the local yellow pages. While most of them offered pretty much the same deal to first-time buyers like himself, he found a few that offered especially low interest rates and low down payments.

He was looking for a loan on a modest three-bedroom frame house, and ended up getting a loan with just 5% interest and $5,000 down! If he'd stopped after the first phone call, he would have paid 8.5% interest with $15,000 down! It just goes to show you, it pays to shop around!

Anatomy of a Mortgage

A typical mortgage has many different parts. What follows is a list of those parts with brief definitions that you can use as a ready reference as you read this chapter.

1. Down payment: the amount of money you must put up to secure your loan.

2. Principal: the amount you are borrowing for your mortgage. This amount does not include interest.

3. Interest rate: a set percentage that is added to the principal. Principal and interest together make up your monthly payment. Interest rates are usually negotiable.

4. Points: one point equals one percent of the total loan amount. Points are charged as fees by lenders to complete your loan. They may be paid up front or in some cases added into your monthly payments. Points are usually negotiable.

3. Term of loan: how long the mortgage lasts. The most common mortgages are 30 years and 15 years, but there are many other options as well.

4. Balloon payment: one big lump sum payment, usually due three to seven years after the mortgage begins. Balloon payments only apply to balloon mortgages. See the section in this chapter on balloon mortgages for details.

5. Mortgage insurance: this is an extra cost required when you get a loan for 90% or more of the purchase price. It is usually added into your monthly payments. A typical fee for mortgage insurance would be $2,500 to $3,500.

6. Up-front costs: these costs include escrow fees, title search costs, appraisal fees, and land survey fees. They vary from lender to lender. This is one area where you can save money by shopping around!

7. Loan repayment schedule: a statement of how much you must pay every month for your mortgage. Loan payments may be the same every month or vary according to changes in interest rates. See the descriptions of different types of mortgages in this chapter for details.

8. Prepayment or late payment penalties: many lenders charge extra money when you make your monthly mortgage payment EARLY or LATE. These penalties vary greatly from lender to lender; always ask for details BEFORE you sign a mortgage contract!

Types of Mortgages

This section provides an easy reference guide to the most common types of mortgages. Specific costs and requirements are discussed for each. Take some time to read over these descriptions. Don't forget, the world of mortgages is a world of possibilities. A little know-how is all you need to find the right mortgage—and you'll get that leading edge right here in this chapter!

Conventional Mortgages

This is the type of loan your parents probably got when they bought the house you grew up in. Conventional mortgages have been around for a long, long time! They usually have the following characteristics:

- They usually require a 20% down payment.
- The term of the loan is 30 years.
- There is one fixed interest rate for the entire term of the loan.
- Monthly payments remain the same for the entire 30 years.

<u>The advantage of conventional loans is their stability.</u> The interest rate and monthly payment amounts are decided up front, and they NEVER CHANGE for the entire 30 years of the loan! Over time, as inflation continues to rise and your payment amount remains the same, your mortgage keeps looking better and better. In fact, every decade people will get more jealous of you and your low monthly payments!

However, the challenge of conventional loans is that big down payment. For a 20% down payment on a $100,000 property, you would need to come up with $20,000 cash—plus cash for the closing costs of an additional $2,000 to $5,000. And that's not counting costs for moving in, decorating, and repairs!

The other problem with conventional loans is the HUGE amount of interest you pay over the term of the loan. If you borrow $100,000 at 8.5% interest and make your payments faithfully month by month for 30 years, you will end up paying a whopping grand total of $176,809 in interest—and that's on top of paying back the principal of $100,000!

So, why on earth would you want a conventional mortgage? Again, the stability factor is very attractive. You always know what your monthly payments will be, and with inflation, your deal gets better over time. The monthly payments are often less than you can get with other types of loans. <u>If you start making more money in a few years, you can always make extra payments to pay off your mortgage sooner—and reduce the total amount you pay in interest.</u> (Just make sure there's not a prepayment penalty before you sign up!)

Also, you can often work out a way to reduce the down payment required on a conventional mortgage, especially in today's economic climate. See the section on how to reduce your down payment at the end of this chapter.

We know a couple with both the husband and wife working—but with three kids and other financial obligations, they could only afford $7,000 for a down payment. Through a friend they found a lender they could trust—someone was willing to work with them and who was sympathetic to their needs. The result? They were able to get a conventional loan with this relatively small down payment—and now they're painting the picket fence around their new front yard!

Shorter Term Conventional Mortgages

If you take out a 15, 20, or 25 year loan, you'll save a bundle in interest over a 30-year conventional loan. See the chart below to compare your interest savings. They're nothing to sneeze at!

Usually 15-year financing offers interest rates .25% to .50% less than 30-year loans. But to get that reduction in interest rates, you end up with much higher monthly payments. That's the trade-off, and that's why 15-year financing is usually not realistic for first-time buyers. Maybe you'll find you can do 20 or 25 year financing, though. If you can swing it, pat yourself on the back—the savings are truly amazing!

Cost Comparison for a $100,000 Conventional Mortgage at 8.5% Interest

Loan Term	30 years	25 years	20 years	15 years
Monthly Payment	$768.91	$805.23	$867.82	$984.74
Interest paid over loan term	$176,809	$141,568	$107,949	$76,880
Total cost of loan	$276,809	$241,568	$207,949	$198,972

Bi-Weekly Mortgages

Essentially, a bi-weekly mortgage is a kind of prepayment plan. Making payments every two weeks is a great way to cut the interest portion of your mortgage payment down to size. Using the same example above of a $100,000 loan at 8.5% interest, you can save nearly $70,000 in interest with a biweekly mortgage.

Also, you can pay off your loan early—usually in about 20 years—rather than the 30 years you face with a conventional mortgage.

If you can handle the discipline of biweekly payments, this is a great way to go. <u>However, you may be better off getting a conventional loan and make larger payments than the lender requires—either monthly or every so often.</u> The reason? You're not locked into the biweekly payment schedule in case you run into financial problems.

Insider's Tip:

BEFORE you start socking away extra money to pay off your mortgage early, <u>do</u> make sure your lender doesn't assess a penalty for prepayments! Some mortgages have prepayment penalties written into the contract. That's one surprise you certainly don't want to wake up to down the road—so read your mortgage carefully before you sign on the dotted line!

Balloon Mortgages

This is a conventional mortgage with a twist. You, the borrower, are offered a low interest rate for the first three to seven years. Then, the principal on the loan is due in full. If you can't come up with that big lump sum payment, you have to refinance the loan.

Some balloon mortgages have built-in refinancing options at five, seven, or ten years. Obviously balloon mortgages can be great if you plan to sell the property before the balloon payment comes due—you get all those years of low interest rates right up front!

But if you're not able to refinance the loan when the lump sum comes due, or if property values are declining, you can run into problems—possibly serious enough problems to result in foreclosure. We do know about one family who lost their home this way—the real estate market had gone sour in their area, and they were unable to sell their home in time before the balloon payment was due.

Proceed with caution—and if you DO decide to take a balloon mortgage, remember to allow PLENTY of time (at least a year or two) to sell the property before the balloon payment comes due—or else, settle on a refinancing plan up front that you feel comfortable with.

Wraparound Mortgages

In this scenario, the seller of the property offers you a second mortgage, usually at a better interest rate than you can get from a lender. You make payments to the seller, who uses part of that money to continue making the monthly payments on his first mortgage.

Wraparounds are usually good for sellers; they can be good for buyers, too, in selected circumstances. As the buyer, you get out of paying points to a commercial lender—plus, you don't have to "qualify" for the loan in the same way that you would if you were using a commercial lender! Now THAT can really make your day!

However, you, the buyer, must ALWAYS protect yourself with a carefully written contract. The risk is: if the seller stops making payments on the first mortgage, the property could be foreclosed upon without you even knowing it! Don't let this scare you off, though. Just get that contract signed, sealed, and delivered—and you could be sitting pretty on a great bargain with a wraparound mortgage!

Insider's Tip:

Stay away from wraparounds that involve third, fourth, fifth, or greater mortgages. These are red flags for buyers—FAR TOO RISKY to waste your time on!

Two-Step Mortgages

In another twist on the conventional mortgage, the two-step pulls in borrowers with a low interest rate for the first five or seven years. At that point, the interest rate is adjusted once, and there it remains for the rest of your 30-year loan.

Here's the catch: there's no telling what interest rates will be five or seven years from now, and there's no cap on what the adjustment will be. Theoretically, in that time interest rates could rise to 12%, 14%, or even higher—and though that probably won't happen, no one's willing to place any bets on it!

But if you plan to move in the next five to seven years, before the adjustment takes place, this option can be a real money-saver! We know one family who did just that. The husband is a traveling salesman, so he's always on the road and being transferred to new regions. The family was able to find a house right smack in the middle of his biggest sales territory. Sure enough, the house was perfect for them for five years—at which time they put the home on the market, sold it in the jiffy, and moved on to the next region—with their pockets lined in greenbacks, we might add, from all the money they saved!

Adjustable Rate Mortgages (ARMs)

These days lenders are pushing ARMs in a big way. With ARMs, the interest rate you pay goes up and down each year according to a set formula, or "index." The interest rate also includes a margin, a fixed percentage that never changes over the life of the loan.

There are a number of indexes that lenders may choose from. Some of the most common ones are:

- 11th District Cost of Funds
- One-year Treasury Securities
- Federal Home Loan Mortgage Corporation (FHLMC) 30-year rates

It's easy to look up these indexes yourself. They are published in many newspapers, including *USA Today's* "Money" section. Be sure to ask lenders for the name of the index being used when you're loan shopping.

With ARMs, the interest rate usually starts low in the first year and then starts to inch up. Adjustments to your interest rate are made at fixed time periods—usually once a year, once every two years, or once every three

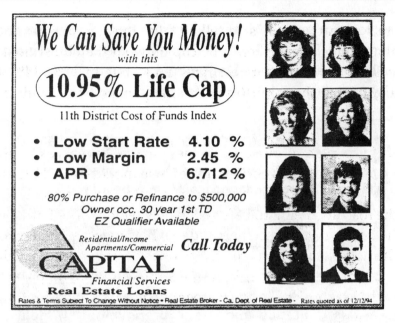

years. (AVOID ARMs that adjust every month or three months—they are NOT a good deal for you, the buyer!)

Most ARMs have an upper limit, or "cap," which protects you by limiting how much your interest rate and monthly payment can increase over the term of the loan. <u>NEVER sign up for an ARM loan without a cap!</u> The cap protects you no matter what happens to interest rates in today's fast-changing economy.

As the borrower, you must shop carefully for ARMs, as for any other loan; <u>the bottom line is that ARMs can work to your advantage, especially if interest rates are falling and if you plan to sell your home within five to ten years.</u>

Insider's tip:

Here's a technique to use when shopping for ARMs: first, look for a fixed payment, conventional loan with the best deal on points and the lowest available interest rate. Then go after an adjustable rate mortgage with the same points and principal amount. Look for an ARM with a lifetime cap of 5% or 6%— meaning that the interest rate can only go up that much more from the initial rate.

Also, look for the best deals on "teaser rates." To get you to sign up, lenders often offer VERY ATTRACTIVE first-year discounts on interest rates! Remember, lenders are out there competing for your business—they WANT and NEED your mortgage business. Make them work for YOU!

How ARMs Stretch Your Buying Power

If you're looking to borrow more money than you can get with conventional mortgages, ARMs may be for you.

• ARMs allow buyers to obtain larger loans than possible with fixed-rate financing.

• Rather than stopping at 30 years, some ARMs offer terms as long as 40 years.

• ARMs are usually assumable by a new buyer at current interest rates—unlike conventional loans.

• ARMs generally encourage prepayments without penalties—which can result in lower monthly costs.

• Even in the worst case scenario, when your ARM goes up the maximum percentage at each readjustment period, you'll often still pay less than you would with fixed-rate financing—at least during in the first five years of the loan.

• An ARM with a conversion clause allows you to switch to a fixed-rate loan—an especially attractive option if interest rates are on their way down.

Buydown Mortgages

If you're interested in buying a brand new home, you'll want to know all about buydown mortgages. Buydown mortgages are often offered by builders who are selling homes in new housing developments. Like ARMs, they feature a movable interest rate. <u>However, there's no surprise factor because the rate changes are all set in advance.</u> You don't get lucky when interest rates go down, but you also don't get burned when rates go up!

Buydowns start out with an interest rate that is well below the prevailing market rate. If the standard rate is currently 8%, a 2-1 buydown loan would offer 6% interest for the first year, 7% interest for the second year, and 8% interest for years three through 30.

The 3-2-1 buydown is one of the most common. If the interest rate were 6% the first year, it would be 7% the second year, 8% the third year, and then 9% for the fourth year and for the rest of the loan term.

Buydowns make it easier for you to qualify to buy a new home. Most lenders use only the first year's monthly payment figure to qualify you—which means you can get into a new home for far less money than you might think! So if it's a new home you really want, don't settle for a fixer-upper—go tour those model homes and get yourself a buydown mortgage instead!

One couple we know was tired of looking only at the rundown, fixer-upper homes in their suburban community. On a whim one day, the wife drove on out to the newest subdivision to look at brand new, 3-bedroom homes. Was she ever surprised to find a great 3-2-1 buydown deal with a maximum interest rate of 8.5%! Now the happy couple spend their weekends at the landscape nursery picking out flowers and shrubs for their great big yard, instead of hammering away on the old clunker they almost bought in the middle of town!

FHA Loans

The Federal Housing Administration (FHA) backs loans that are PERFECT for first-time buyers and other people who can't afford large down payments. Most banks and savings and loan associations offer FHA loans under what is called the 203(b) program. It's possible to get a loan with a down payment as low as 3%! Plus, the interest rate is usually lower than you can get anywhere else.

FHA loans usually have 30-year terms, just like conventional loans, with either fixed or adjustable interest rates. The amount you can borrow is limited, but it's usually sufficient to cover the mortgage you need for a starter home. Sometimes, in more expensive urban and suburban areas, FHA limits are not high enough to provide the mortgage you need. Check with your local lenders for the latest FHA loan limit figures in your area.

Most FHA loans don't come from the FHA itself. Instead, the FHA program insures lenders against default by you. That's why lenders, in turn,

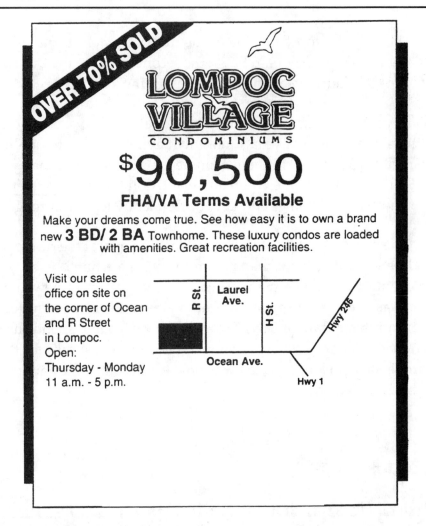

are willing to grant you lower down payments and interest rates. As the borrower, you must pay the mortgage insurance premium—which currently equals 3.8% of your loan amount. This premium can either be paid up front or financed by simply adding it onto your loan. A portion of the premium may be refundable once you pay off your loan.

There are many types of FHA loans. Two of the most common are:

• 203B Mortgage Loan Program. This program has been called the nation's most popular loan. It offers 30-year terms with a low down payment and regular monthly payments for the life of the loan.

• FHA Adjustable Rate Mortgage (ARM). This loan has a low beginning interest rate that may be increased or decreased up to 1 percent each year for a maximum 5 percent increase over the term of the loan.

FHA loans can be used for single-family homes, condominiums and townhouses in FHA-approved complexes, and two-, three-, or four-unit family dwellings. For homes under construction, the FHA requires special paperwork before construction and certain inspections while construction is taking place. FHA loans are NOT available for fixer-upper properties; but you can take advantage of other programs that exist specifically for fixer-uppers (see the chapter on HUD programs in this book).

The appraisal on the home you want to buy—meaning, an official estimate of its worth—must be made by an FHA staff appraiser or an FHA-approved independent appraiser. If the appraiser determines that repairs are required, the property must be reinspected after the repairs have been made.

Insider's Tip:

FHA loans have a reputation for strict requirements and for taking a long time to get approved. You'll need lots of documentation too. Seek out the help of an experienced loan officer. If your lender is a "direct endorsement lender," they are authorized by the FHA to approve your loan if the loan package meets certain requirements. This can definitely help speed up the process!

FHA Loan Profile

1. Down payment: 3% to 5%
2. Interest rate and points: the maximum rate is not set. Rates and points are usually negotiated by lender, borrower, and seller.
3. Term of loan: maximum term is 30 years.
4. Balloon payment: not available with FHA loans.
5. Mortgage insurance: all FHA loans are insured. Borrowers must pay the premium, which equals 3.8% of the loan and is added to your monthly payments.
6. Up-front loan costs: 1% loan origination fee plus certain closing costs. Some closing costs can be financed and paid with monthly payments.
7. Loan repayment schedule: monthly payments can be either fixed or vari-

able, depending on your loan. 203B and 203B2 loans are fixed; some other FHA loans are ARMs (See previous section in this chapter on ARMs, or Adjustable Rate Mortgages.)

8. Prepayment or late payment penalties: prepayments are allowed, though lenders may charge extra interest; late payment penalties are usually 4-5%.

VA Loans

If you've ever served in the armed forces, lucky you! Through Veterans Administration (VA) loans, you're eligible to buy a home with <u>no down payment</u>. You'll have to pay closing costs (usually 5%-7% of the purchase price), plus costs for taxes and escrow accounts, if needed—but that's a smaller price than almost anyone else pays for the privilege of home ownership.

Long ago, the rule was that veterans could only obtain one home loan in their lifetime through the VA. The rules have changed, and this is no longer the case. If you have not purchased a home since December 18, 1989, chances are you'll be eligible!

Eligible individuals include not only veterans who have successfully completed their military service—but also people who have served in certain other government agencies (for example, the Public Health Service). Unmarried widows of veterans and spouses of POWs and MIAs are also eligible. Veterans who have served in two or more wars may have TWO full entitlements! Those currently on active duty must serve 181 consecutive days to be eligible for an entitlement.

If you qualify, you need to round up two forms: Form DD 214, which is given upon your release from military service, plus VA Form 26-1880, "Request for Certificate of Eligibility." Ask for these forms at your local VA office. The office will then give you a "Certificate of Eligibility," which you then take with you on your shopping trips to various lenders.

Properties eligible for VA loans include single-family homes, condos, townhouses, and two-, three-, and four-unit family dwellings. Loans on new homes are available if certain guidelines are followed during construction.

The appraisal on your prospective home must be conducted by a VA-approved appraiser. This individual must complete the Certificate of Reasonable Value (CRV), which is the VA appraisal form. The amount of your mortgage loan for the property cannot exceed the amount stated on the CRV.

A word of caution: while no money down sounds great, it does mean that your mortgage will be hefty, as well as your monthly payments. You may be stuck with a higher interest rate as well. But no money down can still be worth it, especially if it means you can buy your first home NOW!

(Veterans take note: you also qualify for the FHA's 203B2 Mortgage Loan Program. This program is very similar to the 203B program described above, except that your down payment can be EVEN LESS! All veterans with 180 days of active duty service are eligible.)

VA Loan Profile

1. Down payment: no down payment if buyer meets VA and lender guidelines.

2. Interest rate: cannot exceed the maximum permitted by law—but is very often lower than rates you'll find anywhere else.

3. Term of loan: maximum term is 30 years.

4. Balloon payment: no balloon payment.

5. Mortgage insurance: loans are guaranteed by federal government at no cost to you.

6. Up-front loan costs: fees may include a 1% loan origination fee, .5% to 1.25% VA funding fee, and other closing costs allowed by the VA. Buyers don't pay for the appraisal or points.

7. Loan repayment schedule: choice of fixed payments, buydown loans, or ARMs.

8. Prepayment or late payment penalties: no prepayment penalties; late payment penalties at 4%.

Private Mortgage Insurance

What's a cash-poor borrower to do if you're not a veteran, and if you live in a high-cost urban or suburban area where FHA loans don't offer enough money for the mortgage you need?

Enter Private Mortgage Insurance, or PMI. With PMI, first-time buyers can get financing with <u>as little as 5 percent down.</u> PMI is insurance that protects the lender if you default on the loan. As the borrower, you pay the premiums for this coverage. Ask your lender for details on this money-saving option!

PMI premiums vary depending on the size of your down payment. Usually the payment involves a percentage of the principal amount on the loan up front, plus a smaller percentage paid monthly over time. There is also another payment option called "lump sum PMI," where you add the premium to the loan amount and pay the entire lump sum back over time. Again, ask your friendly lender for details about PMI and how it can help you buy a home for less!

Assumptions

Assumptions can be a real gold mine for buyers. Sometimes you can assume the owner's existing mortgage, meaning that you take over his or her monthly payments. You may even be able to assume their old interest rate as well! This almost always means a better deal for you, the buyer— you might even find an interest rate EVEN LESS than the going rate of between 8% to 9%!

Not all loans are assumable. Most loans made prior to 1980 ARE assumable, but the disadvantage is that their balances can be so small that assuming them isn't worth it to you.

A better bet is FHA loans, which can be assumed after the previous owner has held the property for just one year. Because FHA loans require less than 5% down, they usually represent a substantial chunk of a home's financing—at interest rates you'll be only too happy to take over from the current owner!

Many loans made in recent years are <u>qualified assumptions,</u> which mean that you, the new borrower, must meet the approval of the old lender. This may be easiest in the case of ARMs—since with ARMs, interest rates always stay up-to-date.

The bottom line is that assumptions are a GREAT way to get into the home of your choice. <u>Sometimes it's easier to assume an old loan than to go out and get a new one!</u> Keep your eyes open for assumable loans and take advantage of the great opportunity they represent to SAVE YOU MONEY!

Good Old Mom and Dad Mortgages

Your parents may be among those lucky folks who bought real estate decades ago, at prices and interest rates we can only dream about today. They may now own their home free and clear, or close to it, and their property may have appreciated astronomically in value.

If this profile fits your parents, they are in an excellent position to help you buy a home. In fact, over a third of first-time homebuyers get help from their parents in some way or another.

This help can take several forms:

• An outright cash gift from your parents to you. Lenders will want to see a "gift letter" that shows all demands for repayment are waived.
• A refinancing deal where your parents refinance their own home and pay for your new home in cash—giving you much more favorable terms than you could get elsewhere. You then make monthly payments to your folks.
• A life insurance deal where your parents take out a life insurance policy worth the amount of the mortgage. When they die, you can pay off your mortgage with these non-taxable insurance proceeds.

We know lots of folks who borrowed the down payment on their homes from their parents. Most times this is just a matter of between $5,000 and $10,000—an amount that many parents won't even miss! Even if your parents want to be paid back at some point, you can often reach an agreement to do so over a period of time—and they may even agree to little or no interest! One thing's for sure—it can't hurt to ask, and you might be surprised at how generous your folks can be!

> ### Insider's Tip:
>
> Outright financial gifts can carry a BIG tax bite. It's absolutely essential that you and your parents consult tax, real estate, and life insurance professionals BEFORE making, or receiving, any large gifts like those described above.

Cut Your Down Payment Down to Size

We already talked about the importance of saving for a down payment in the last chapter. While savings of your own are a definite plus, <u>don't let the lack of 10%-20% of the purchase price for a down payment stand between you and your dream of home ownership!</u>

If you have good credit, somewhat regular income, and even minimal savings, you should be able to buy a home with a down payment of $500 to $3,000—<u>or even no down payment at all!</u> Here are some creative solutions to the down payment dilemma:

• **Find a desperate seller**—someone who wants and needs to sell their property NOW. Often these people will agree to "take back" a percentage of the purchase price as a loan to you instead of getting a large cash down payment.

• **Consider equity sharing,** where you bring in a partner to help make the down payment and share other costs. You make monthly payments, keep the property in good condition, and make improvements while you live there. When you sell the property, you divide up the profits with your partner.

• **Borrow the down payment from your credit union.** This loan will probably be a financial challenge to pay off, but it may be better than waiting forever to save for a down payment—especially if you really feel you've found the right property.

• **Lease with an option to buy.** Find a house that is up for lease and make a deal! Have your attorney draw up an agreement that locks in the purchase price right away and sets a fixed date at which you will exercise your option.

• **Find a co-signer for your mortgage loan.** You need someone with a strong financial profile. Parents often make good co-signers. This is an especially good strategy for people who have the basic qualifications for a loan, but who live in areas where home prices are just too high.

• **Watch for special offers by local savings and loans.** Through these programs, qualified buyers can sometimes obtain mortgages with as little as 5% down!

• **Investigate tax-free bonds**—a solution developed by local and state governments to provide low-interest loans to low-income people. These loans feature interest rates below those charged by conventional lenders and enable you to take out a larger mortgage than you could otherwise.

Loan Profile Chart

Use the blank Loan Profile Chart on the next page when you're in the process of shopping for loans. Make copies of the chart and fill in a new one for each lender you visit. This method will help you keep track of the features of many different loans. Shop and compare, and you'll get the most value for your money!

Remember to visit more than one lender! You'll be amazed at how many differences you discover from lender to lender. You'll find some important ways to save money in the process. For example, even saving 1/2 point on your interest rate can add up into TREMENDOUS savings over the life of your mortgage!

When all is said and done, buying a home is alot like buying a car. To get the best deal on a new car, you go to several different dealerships. You get one dealer to give you a price, then you go to the next dealer and try to get them to beat that price.

You can apply the EXACT SAME TECHNIQUE to buying a home! As you become familiar with mortgages by calling different lenders, you'll soon reach the point where you can be tough at the bargaining table. That's when you can use some of the tips in our next chapter—Chapter 4, Your Strategy. And don't forget—if you can buy a car, you can buy a house! It's that simple!

Loan Profile Chart

Name of Lending Institution: _____

Address: _____

Phone number: _____

Name of Loan Officer: _____

Type of Loan (conventional, FHA, VA, ARM, etc.): _____

_____

Down payment: _____

Interest rate: _____

Points: _____

Term of loan: _____

Balloon payment: _____

Mortgage insurance: _____

Up-front loan costs: _____

Loan repayment schedule: _____

Prepayment or late payment penalties: _____

Chapter 4:
Your Strategy

Now that you've got your financial picture in focus and a basic understanding of mortgage loans, you're ready to find the home of your dreams. This chapter is about planning your search, selecting the home that's best for YOU, dealing with real estate agents and brokers, how to price a home, and how to place an offer or bid! Remember, YOU CAN DO IT! Somebody's got to buy the great bargain homes we're talking about in this book—and it might as well be you!

Finding the PERFECT Bargain Home

Now let's do a mental exercise together. Close your eyes and picture your ideal home in your mind. See the outside of the house, the yard, what the front door looks like, and each of the rooms inside, one by one. Visit the living room, dining room, kitchen, den, bathrooms, bedrooms, all of it! Don't forget the basement or attic, if you want one!

Then open your eyes. The picture you've created is yours to keep forever. You'll always carry it with you. Now, as you go house hunting in the real world with your eyes wide open, look for the homes that are CLOSE to your ideal. Look past the surface details. For example, it doesn't matter if the carpeting is bad—carpeting is one of the easiest and cheapest things to fix! If the paint is peeling, so what—you can slap on a new coat of paint in no time flat!

Even though we'd like to believe otherwise, the perfect home usually exists only in our minds. Even the wealthiest people make trade-offs or compromises to get some features at the expense of others. You'll find the same is true of your own house hunting. In fact, being able to look past surface appearances is . . .

Your Key to Success!

The key to buying a discount home is to snap up a house that LOOKS like a clunker—but really isn't. You want a house that, once it's painted and cleaned up, will be worth FAR MORE than it is now. We're not talking about a house that needs a new foundation, or all new plumbing and electrical wiring, or any other major renovations—we're just talking about cosmetic repairs.

In fact, your ideal house is a neglected house in a good neighborhood. You get it for a great price, fix it up, and then you have a house that you can resell any time you like and make a HEFTY profit!

Always remember that you MUST stay away from bad neighborhoods! The idea here is not to put your safety at risk—nor do you want to be the first person on the block to fix your home up nicely. The way the neighborhood as a whole looks determines property values—and it won't matter if you've got the nicest home on the block when you can't sell it for anywhere near what you paid for it!

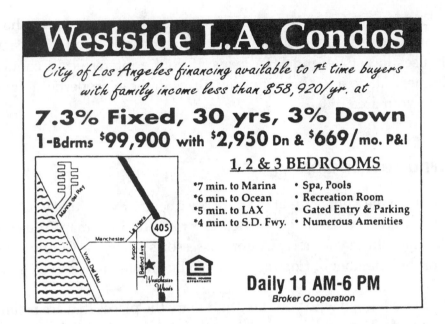
Back to Basics

Now let's get back to basics. Ask yourself these four questions:

• What type of home do I prefer and will best meet my needs—single family home, condominium, townhouse, duplex, etc.?

• What style home do I prefer—Victorian, Colonial, Ranch, A-frame, Contemporary, etc.?

• How many bedrooms and baths are an absolute necessity?

• Do I anticipate any changes in my income or lifestyle over the next 5, 15, and 20 years? If so, will these changes affect the kind of house I need today?

Townhouses Vs. Condominiums: What's the Difference?

Townhouses and condominiums share some things in common. Both are usually part of a complex that includes common areas and amenities like a clubhouse, pool, tennis courts, and open space. They also both charge monthly fees for the maintenance of common areas.

The difference is that when you buy a townhouse, you own all of the actual structure, inside and out—including the walls, roof, and floor. With a condominium, you own only what's INSIDE the walls.

Condominiums can be harder to finance than single family homes. Townhouses are usually easier to finance than condos—and it's easier for townhouses to get VA and FHA loans. If you're interested in condos or townhomes, talk to a Realtor who specializes in these properties to get the scoop for your area.

Planning Your Search

Your quest for the right home at the right price begins by limiting your search to a specific area. So let's begin by defining that area on a map! You can get oversize maps from your local County Assessor's office, the County Clerk's office, or the Chamber of Commerce—even bus route maps can be good.

Now sit down with your map and mark the places that are meaningful in your life. These might include your place of work, the shopping centers you frequent, and the schools your kids attend. Somewhere in between these places you'll find neighborhoods that are worthy of your consideration. Scout them out by driving around. If you need additional help identifying good neighborhoods, find a Realtor to help guide you—remember, their services are free, and their advice can be fantastic!

We have a friend who was at a total loss. She needed to find a house within 20 miles of the manufacturing plant where she works. She thought she'd seen every possible neighborhood. But lo and behold, she finally called a Realtor in desperation. That Realtor drove her straight out to a neighborhood behind a big shopping center that she had never seen before! Now she owns a great little 2-bedroom home there—and when it's time to go grocery shopping or rent a video, all she has to do is walk across the street !

Finding "Good" Neighborhoods

How can you tell if the neighborhood is "good"? Good neighborhoods are places where the homes are well maintained, or where renovations are in progress. The streets are clean and the stores are busy. Make it a point to get out of your car and meet some people in a neighborhood that appeals to you. You might strike up a conversation at the local coffee shop or in line at the store. Find out how safe the neighborhood is, how people feel about the neighborhood, the neighborhood's history, changes in the recent past, and any other issues—from taxes to factors like flooding or other natural disasters—that might affect your decision.

What About Amenities?

Look at the amenities that are within easy driving distance. Is the neighborhood within a half-hour drive of a major urban center? How about shopping, recreation, an airport, and access to public transportation? Homes with easy access to most of these features have the potential for good resale value.

Try to limit your search to an area of 2,000 homes or less. This equals about one square mile in the suburbs or 150 square blocks in the city. By limiting your search, you'll get to know one area extremely well. You'll become acquainted with people in the area, and soon you'll be one of the first to know when bargain homes go on the market.

Insider's Tip:

Look for homes in areas where prices aren't high now, but where they are expected to be high in the future. Future growth will make your home increase in value—and your investment will repay itself many times over.

Key signs of future growth include: new roads, office construction, shopping malls, or schools. Experts in the community's zoning and planning office should be able to provide you with projections for the next 5 to 10 years. "Official statements" from recent bond issues are also a good source of information about future growth in the community of your choice. Ask to see copies of these at your local zoning and planning office.

About Real Estate Professionals

Now let's talk about your friendly real estate professionals—real estate agents, Realtors and Brokers. To keep this section brief, we'll refer to them all as Realtors. Here's a rule of thumb: Realtors are great if you choose them, and not so great if they choose you!

Realtors primarily work for sellers. After all, it's sellers who usually pay their commissions. If you are a buyer and find yourself being pursued by an aggressive Realtor, beware! You may get an earful about properties you don't really want—or even be dragged off to look at them!

The Traits of a Good Realtor

On the other hand, the right Realtor has the know-how to lead you past the duds to the home that's right for you. Good Realtors know their community like the back of their hand. They can rattle off current home values; show you properties in a given area and price range; describe the features of those properties in detail; provide you with information about school districts, property taxes, lot sizes, and utilities; supply documents such as surveys, floor plans, and lease agreements; and describe financing options, current rates, and terms. Now what other person could possibly do ALL THIS for you?

Again, however, we must repeat that most real estate agents and brokers work for SELLERS. They have no obligation to protect your best interests. They will not represent you in any way or negotiate on your behalf. So it's up to you to use their knowledge for your own benefit.

A friend of ours was new to the area and had to find a home and start a new job at the same time. He asked around his new workplace and got the names of a couple of Realtors. The first one wasn't any help at all, but the second one took up his cause and found him a house within a week's time! He was able to send for his family and keep his boss happy too—and he couldn't have done it without someone who knew the area like that Realtor!

Use More Than One Realtor—At First

When you're first getting to know an area, it's a good strategy to seek out more than one Realtor. In fact, you should make a point of "interviewing" various Realtors and tapping into their knowledge about the area. Stick with Realtors who are full-time agents with established companies. These are the professionals who keep up with every aspect of the complex real estate market.

If you find a Realtor you feel you can trust, you may want to let him or her show you properties exclusively from then on. Realtors are touchy about potential buyers who play the field. They want to feel that they have us in their pocket—after all, their income depends in part on our loyalty! So our suggestion to you is to give the right Realtor that courtesy.

Buyer Brokers

There is a relatively new breed of Realtors afoot known as the buyer broker. This realtor actually DOES work for you, the buyer. Buyer brokers can either help you find a property, negotiate on your behalf, or both. You pay them an hourly fee or a set fee, such as a finder's fee. Because this represents an extra cost, you must decide whether your particular circumstances justify the extra expense.

Location, Location, Location!

Once you've established your target area and your target price, you're ready to zero in on actual homes. Which brings us to the most important factor in looking for discount real estate: location, location, location! Look at every home with an eagle eye. Visit a house you're serious about at different times of day, on different days of the week. Observe the neighborhood. Ask questions like these:

• Is there a school nearby that lets out packs of noisy children during recess?
• Is the house on a hill, a corner, or a busy street?
• Are sidewalks and driveways paved?
• How's the landscaping around the house?
• Are the size and shape of the lot an asset or a liability?
• Do trains go by in the middle of the night?
• What about airstrips—is the house right under a busy flight path?

Other factors that can affect the desirability of a house include zoning regulations, excessive taxes, deed restrictions, and city or county easements. Ask about ALL of these items if you're serious about placing an offer on a particular house!

How to Price the Home You Want

The easiest way to judge the asking price on the house you want is to conduct your own market analysis. In other words, find out what similar homes in the same area have sold for in recent months. What we mean by "the same area" is very specific. It means down the block, around the corner, or the next street over. The farther away you get from the home itself, the less relevant is the cost comparison.

The most important factor for your cost comparison is size. What is the size of the lot, and how many square feet are included in the house? Keep in mind that different people include different items in the square footage total. Some might include garage space, balconies, and unfinished basements in the total to make it sound bigger. <u>Always ask specifically what "living space" includes when you are given a square footage figure!</u>

We heard about one house where this square footage factor became a real fiasco! The house was listed as a 3-bedroom with over 3,500 square feet of living area. Turns out that the largest bedroom was 9 x 12. A three-car garage was included in the square footage figure, and each of the garage units was bigger than those bedrooms! Not only that, there was a crawl space included in the square footage as well!

```
┌─────────────────────────────────────────────────┐
│                  Insider's Tip                   │
│                                                  │
│  A home inspection is one of the most important  │
│  things you can do before buying a home! See     │
│  Chaper 18 for a complete checklist of potential │
│  problems to identify BEFORE you place your      │
│  offer.                                          │
└─────────────────────────────────────────────────┘
```

Placing an Offer

You've found the home you want. You know the home's listing price and terms. You've done your research on similar properties and have a sense of the real market value of the home you want.

Now you're ready to make an offer. You are free to make **ANY OFFER YOU WISH.** Don't feel bound by the listing price. <u>Generally you want to make your offer as low as possible without being completely unreason-</u>

able. What that means depends on the status of the sellers and on the property itself. Sellers who are desperate to unload their homes may accept an especially low offer from you. On the other hand, too low an offer may turn the sellers off and make it harder for you to continue negotiating.

Don't forget that you can negotiate on points as well as the asking price. You can negotiate on some other items as well. See the section on "Closing Costs" below for details.

The seller's Realtor will convey your offer to the seller. The seller may either accept your offer as is, reject your offer completely, or make a few changes and send it back to you as a counteroffer. Then you have the same three options: acceptance of the counteroffer, rejection, or another counteroffer. The game continues until an agreement is reached or one of the parties calls it quits.

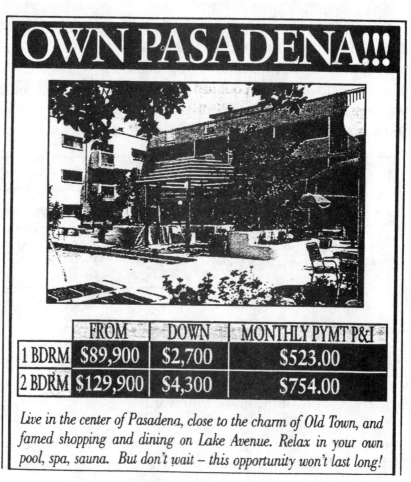

OWN PASADENA!!!

	FROM	DOWN	MONTHLY PYMT P&I
1 BDRM	$89,900	$2,700	$523.00
2 BDRM	$129,900	$4,300	$754.00

Live in the center of Pasadena, close to the charm of Old Town, and famed shopping and dining on Lake Avenue. Relax in your own pool, spa, sauna. But don't wait – this opportunity won't last long!

Negotiate on Closing Costs

These costs may look small at first, but they add up fast. You can expect closing costs to equal 5% to 7% of the total purchase price. Closing costs include:

- Loan origination fees
- Title search costs
- Appraisal fees
- Land survey fees
- Points

Each point on a mortgage is equal to 1 percent of the total loan amount. Most lenders charge 2 to 3 points to cover the costs of processing the loan and a credit check.

You can reduce your closing costs by shopping around for the best deals on costs that aren't fixed—for example, surveys, appraisals, and legal fees. Also, try to get sellers to share expenses like the land survey, title search, termite inspection, and engineer's report. Remember that NO POINTS are charged if you can find a seller who's willing to finance the purchase. You can also avoid paying loan processing fees and credit checks this way. If the seller wants a credit report on you, you can obtain one quickly and easily (See Chapter 3). We know many satisfied buyers who have gone this route. One fellow was able to negotiate with the seller and get a good interest rate with a 10-year payoff! Can you imagine owning your own home, free and clear, in just 10 years? Sure, he's had to spend some time to fix it up, but he's done almost all the work himself—and he's happy as a clam at high tide!

Buying at Auction

Buying properties at private auctions, government auctions, or other foreclosure auctions is another GREAT source of bargain homes—and it has its own special strategy for success!

First, scan the newspaper for ads announcing the sale of these properties. Then, when you see an interesting property, call the number listed in the ad. Try to examine any documents pertaining to the property from sources like the county courthouse, the owner, and the sponsor of the auction.

At the same time, speak with a lender and get your financing lined up—so when you walk into the auction, you'll know exactly the highest amount you can bid. You'll also want to do your own inspection and/or appraisal of the property.

What to Expect at the Auction

At the auction, properties come up for bidding one by one. An opening bid is announced for each property. This figure is also known as the "upset price." Some auctions are conducted by verbal bidding, where bidders simply call out their offers. Other auctions use sealed written bids, where the envelopes are opened and the property goes to the highest bidder.

If you are the lucky highest bidder, you must hand over the down payment right then and there—which is usually 10% of the bid amount. You will be issued a certificate of sale on the spot. The balance will be due within a set time period, usually within 30 days after the auction.

It's important to remember two things about foreclosures: they are sold "as is," meaning that there are no guarantees that the property is in good condition; and if there are tenants on the property, the task of moving them out falls on you, the new owner.

The good news is it's not unusual to find yourself the ONLY BIDDER who shows up for an auction! We know a family man who had his eye on an auction property and got all set to place his bid. The morning of the auction, there had been a huge snowstorm. He got out his four-wheel-drive pickup and blasted through the snowdrifts to the County Courthouse. Sure enough, he was the only guy who made it—and his lowball bid was the winner!

How Much To Bid?

The offer you make depends on WHERE and HOW you plan to get your financing. You can make lower offers on FHA foreclosures than on VA foreclosures, for example. As a general rule, bid between 30%-50% of the property's fair market value—and never bid more than 75%! See the table below for bidding guidelines according to the agency offering the property.

Standard Bids for Auction Sales of Single-Family Homes

Agency	Ideal Bid (% of Fair Market Value)
Fannie Mae/Freddie Mac	45-55%
FDIC	30-55%
GSA	20-30%
HUD	35-45%
IRS	35-45%
Probate sales	40-50%
State Surplus	25-35%
Tax Sales	20-30%
VA	60-70%

What's Next?

Now you've got some insight into the strategies of home buying and how to make them work for you. You're ready to learn about all the great government agencies and programs out there that exist to help YOU buy an incredible bargain home!

Chapters 5 through 17 take you on a tour through these programs and opportunities. You'll be amazed at the deals and how easy it is to take advantage of them! So sit back and get comfortable, take it a chapter at a time, and get ready for the excitement of picking and choosing the programs that are right for you!

Chapter 5:
Put HUD To Work for You

Now you're about to discover one of the best sources of discount homes in America today—HUD, or the Department of Housing and Urban Development! HUD dates back to the early 1960s, when the United States Congress decided that every family in the U.S. deserves decent, affordable housing. Congress also demanded equal housing opportunity for all. HUD was established in 1965 to carry out these congressional mandates.

Today, nearly 30 years later, HUD is still going strong! You can benefit from HUD in two ways. First, HUD offers GREAT DEALS on bargain properties for sale. Second, HUD sponsors affordable housing programs in communities all across the country! These programs are especially geared for low to moderate income home buyers. In this chapter you'll get an overview of HUD property sales and programs that will help you chart a course to INCREDIBLE homes at UNBELIEVABLE prices!

HUD Property Sales

Basically, HUD sells properties that have defaulted on government loans. These properties are repossessed and made available to the general public—that means you and me! They are typically sold at public auction through qualified real estate brokers. At any given time, HUD owns from 10,000 to 50,000 properties in various communities across the nation—and one of them could soon be yours!

Just Look at These Deals!

The good news is, HUD homes usually sell **BELOW MARKET VALUE!** Also, interest rates are usually low and other costs (e.g. transfer fees, other closing costs) are minimal. To get an idea of these low, low prices, see the sample list of HUD properties in Southern California on the next page. How would you like to get a one-bedroom condo for $45,000, or a three-bedroom house for $90,000? You get the idea—HUD is truly a wonderland of bargains!

Who Handles These Sales?

HUD sales are handled through your friendly local real estate broker. Call around and ask the Realtors in your area if they handle HUD sales. They will obtain a list of properties for you from the local HUD office, and then they will go with you to visit the properties. Your broker will have the keys to the houses you want to see, as well as all the information you need to complete the transaction.

Please note: As an individual home buyer, you <u>must</u> go through a broker to buy a HUD home. But you can certainly call your regional office for more information about HUD programs. A list of regional HUD offices is included in Appendix A at the back of this book. Plus you can refer to your companion book, Volume II, for current property listings!

Get Property Lists from HUD Fast!

When you call the HUD Office located closest to you, you may be surprised to find that their phone system is totally computerized. This can be an advantage. For instance, we called the Los Angeles Field Office, and within minutes we had a property list faxed right to our offices! Other HUD offices may not be as advanced, but one phone call is all you need to get started in the great and wondrous world of HUD—and you'll be that much closer to owning your own home! (Plus, check Volume II for current listings NOW!)

HUD's Affordable Housing Programs

HUD has a unique way of providing funds for affordable housing programs. In most cases, HUD gives general guidelines to State and local governments—and then leaves it to them to design affordable housing programs that meet the needs of your particular area.

HUD HOMES

●NEW LISTINGS●

Bids accepted until 4:30 p.m., December 19, 1994
Bids opened Tuesday, December 20, 1994, at 9 a.m.

Available To Owner/Occupants Only
Some Properties may Be Available To Investors---Call HUD.

HUD#	ADDRESS	PRICE	FHA
	BRIAN HEAD		
142191	Unit 4, Bldg. A.	$47,400	YES
	645 Sq, Ft., 2 Bdrms., 1 Bath		
	Condo, LBP		
	OGDEN		
319366		$47,500	YES
	938 Sq. Ft., 2 Bdrms., 1 Ba.,		
	1 carport, rambler, LBP		
	$450.00 floor allowance		
195068		$60,700	YES
	889 Sq. Ft., 2/2 Bdrms., 1 Ba.,		
	1 Gar., Rambler, LBP $1,700 F&P Alw.		
	VERNAL		
160263		$21,500	NO
	1047 Sq. FT., 2 Bedrms., 1 Ba., Rambler,		
	LBP, Acreage, Septic NOT inspected,		
	Structural Damage		

<u>Repair Escrow Properties</u>

		"AS IS"	ESCR	FHA
	OGDEN			
280018		$53,000	3,520	$55,200
	1102 Sq. Ft., 2 Bdrms., 1Ba.,			
	1 Gar., Rambler, LBP			

●EXTENDED LISTINGS●

Bids accepted until 3:00 daily
Bids opened at 3:15 pm daily

	BRIAN HEAD		
220094		$29,900	NO
	456 Sq. Ft., 2 Bdrms., 1 Ba.,		
	2 space covered parking, Condo		
	FT. DUCHESENE		
232791		$52,400	YES
	1161 Sq. Ft., 3/1 Bdrms., 2 Ba.,		
	2 Gar., Tri Level, P Alw. $2,500		

HUD tries to meet the short-term goal of increasing the supply of affordable housing. HUD also has a long-term goal of building partnerships between State government, local government, private organizations, and nonprofit organizations to meet the housing needs of low and very low-income residents. These programs are individually tailored to fit each community.

Here's a great example of what HUD money and local ingenuity can do! We know about one HUD-sponsored program that built <u>17 brand-new condominiums specifically for ARTISTS with low incomes.</u> HUD joined with a private, nonprofit arts organization in the community to make this project happen. Residents who qualified were able to get loans at a mere 3% interest—plus, if they didn't have the $5,000 down payment, they could BORROW that, too! Which means that most of those 17 happy individuals were able to buy a condo with practically no money at all!

How To Find HUD Programs Near You

There are a variety of ways to go about researching HUD programs in your area. First, you must be aware that HUD accommodates three different types of buyers: *First-time home buyers* who are looking for a home they will live in; *Investors* who are looking for great deals in their local housing market; and *Brokers* who want to help buyers find the deal that's just right for them.

When you contact one of the sources below, please let them know whether you are a *First-time home buyer, Investor* or *Broker.* This will help put you immediately in touch with the person who can help you!

Insider's Tip:

First-time home buyer is defined by the Housing and Community Development Act of 1992 as follows: "Any low-income household (below 80% of the area median income, as determined by HUD) that has not owned a home in the previous three years." <u>Exceptions are made in certain programs, though, so always ask for details!</u>

Five Ways to Find HUD Programs

You have basically five options to find out about HUD programs in your area, and we'll cover each of them one by one:

- Your Telephone Book
- HUD Homes Hot Line
- American Communities Home Information Center
- HUD USER
- HUD Regional and Field Offices

Your Telephone Book

Sometimes, the best place to start is with your telephone book. Let your fingers do the walking right into the County or City government section and look for something like "COMMUNITY DEVELOPMENT & HOUSING DEPARTMENT." Give them a call and ask to speak to the person in charge of HUD programs or other programs for first-time home buyers in your area.

The more specific you can be in describing the home you are looking for, the easier this process will be for you. But also remember that many of these HUD programs have very specific requirements. Part of your job is to find out what these requirements are. You may find a local HUD program you never knew existed that is just right for you! It helps to be flexible and patient—by all means, do everything you can to keep your stress level down while you search for your new home!

HUD Homes Hot Line

You can also call the HUD HOMES HOT LINE. They will send you a FREE brochure that outlines HUD programs that you'll surely be interested in, whether you are a first-time home buyer, an investor or a broker.

HUD HOMES HOT LINE
(800) 769-4483

American Communities Home Information Center

This is a new government agency that has been in existence since 1992. It's a FREE information service! If they can't answer your question directly, they will put you in touch with someone who can—or, they'll do the research and get back to you. Their number is:

American Communities Home Information Center
(800) 998-9999

When we called, there was a friendly information specialist ready and willing to answer our questions about HUD's programs in the Community Planning and Development area. They have documents describing the various HUD programs in great detail. We like to think of them as the "one stop shopping center" for HUD. They explained that they see themselves as the middleman between HUD programs and potential home buyers.

To give you an idea of the different types of programs HUD offers, we'll outline just a few. These programs are all funded with the help of HUD money and administered by local Community Development Departments. So like we said earlier, call your local Community Development Department for more specific information about these and other HUD programs!

Community Development Block Grants

Funds for Community Development Block Grants are distributed every year to communities all across the country. Each community then develops local housing programs aimed towards neighborhood revitalization and improved community facilities and services. HUD states that these programs must either benefit low to moderate income persons or help prevent and eliminate slums.

HOPE: Single Family Homes for Everyone!

This national program stands for "Home Ownership for People Everywhere," and the name is the goal of this great program. Local HOPE programs sell single family properties to eligible families and individuals at VERY affordable prices. The program is available ONLY to families and individuals who are first-time home buyers with an income at or below 80% of the area's median income (adjusted for family size). The HOPE program also ensures that monthly housing payments are no more than 30% of the adjusted monthly income of the family or individual.

The Community Development Block Grants and HOPE programs are programs of the American Communities Home Information Center. To find out more about these programs and others offered in your area, call the American Communities Home Information Center at:

(800) 998-9999

HUD USER

If you want to help improve housing and strengthen community development in your area, this is the place for you! HUD USER is sponsored by the HUD's Office of Policy Development and Research (PD&R). This is a research service and clearing house for information. Reference Specialists are just waiting for your toll-free call, and they can provide a wealth of resources and services, such as:

<u>Audiovisual programs</u> designed as "how-to" guides on subjects like "Home Conversion" and "Lead Based Paint Abatement Training for Supervisors and Contractors." Most of these videotapes show case studies of successful programs developed across the country with the help of HUD funds.

<u>Resource Guides</u> which provide up-to-date information on housing and development. They can save you time and money by identifying resource materials available through HUD on topics like "Directory of Information Resources in Housing and Development, Third Edition, 1993" and "Housing Special Populations: A Resource Guide."

To contact HUD User, call or write:
HUD User
PO Box 6091
Rockville, MD 20850
(800) 245-2691

HUD Regional and Field Offices

HUD has divided the United States into 10 regions, and there are a number of field offices within each region. These offices handle all the work at the local level. By giving the office closest to you a call, you find out who to contact in your own neck of the woods for the most up-to-date HUD opportunities. You'll find a complete list of offices in Appendix A at the back of this book!

In Closing . . .

These are just some of the many, many programs currently active through HUD. In your search to purchase an affordable home, you'll most certainly want to contact your local HUD office to see if any of their programs match your current needs!

Remember, HUD's philosophy is that when families become homeowners, they build better, stronger neighborhoods. HUD programs allow eligible families and individuals to develop a stake in their own homes and, in turn, their communities. So, take some time to explore these programs—you'll be glad you did!

Chapter 6: Bank Foreclosures and REOs

We've all heard it said that "One man's ceiling is another man's floor"—and perhaps nowhere in the real estate game is this more true than in the area of foreclosure sales.

This saying applies because *at no other time* in the history of real estate deals has this way of obtaining bargain properties been so common as in today's troubled, topsy-turvy economy! As more and more people find themselves unable to make their monthly house payments, the number of properties being "taken back" by lenders grows larger every day.

This is bad news for homeowners—but fantastic news for you, the home buyer! NOW is the best time in real estate history to make your move, because you can literally get in on the ground floor, usually paying far less than market value for the home of your choice. Then you can sit back and wait for the right moment to sell, knowing that you'll make the maximum return on your investment. In today's real estate market, the sky's the limit!

This chapter will give you an overview of foreclosures—how to identify, research, locate, and actually bid on foreclosed property. Please remember that laws regarding foreclosures vary greatly from state to state, so be sure to learn about the laws specific to your state before you actually make a bid on a great-looking property. You'll find many extremely helpful people along the way—like real estate agents, brokers, and state officials—who can provide you with this information as you learn about the foreclosures.

Financing IS Possible

You may have heard that foreclosure properties require cash up front. While it is true that foreclosure properties are often sold for cash at public auctions, you don't always need a "small suitcase" full of greenbacks to take advantage of these great deals. Creative financing can be arranged, especially for REO sales (more on these in a minute!)

Many foreclosed properties can be obtained for prices far less than fair market value because lenders are anxious to cut their losses and get their mortgage money circulating again. As the buyer, you are the one who stands to benefit from these low prices. We know a family of six who thought they could never afford to move from their two-bedroom bungalow into a larger home. Weren't they surprised when they found out that through a foreclosure sale, they could own a clean, decent four-bedroom home with a big backyard for two thirds of the regular market price!

Get to Know the Market

Foreclosure properties sold at public auctions are typically turned around FAST. Once you find a property, you won't have much time to study the market and learn if it's a good deal or not—so you'll be ahead of the game if you start getting familiar with foreclosure procedures and foreclosure properties NOW! That way you'll be prepared to act quickly once you find the property you really want.

Real estate sales depend on a well-oiled machine—and by that, we mean lots of people talking to lots of people about who's selling what and who's buying what. You'd be surprised how readily people will want to talk with you about these things. In fact, you may have a hard time shutting them up once they get started!

Realtors can be a great help to you in this area. Since Realtors never know where their next sale may come from, they'll bend over backwards to help you if they know what you're looking for. But before you spread the word on the street, you need to become familiar with exactly . . .

What is a Foreclosure?

Simply put, foreclosure is what happens when monthly mortgage payments are not made on time. As a result, the lender "takes the property back." This is a legal action, and there is not much flexibility in the process.

When a borrower gets behind in their mortgage payments, the lender will send written requests for payment. If the payments aren't made, the lender will eventually send warnings about possible foreclosure. If payments are still not made, the lender will enter a "Notice of Default" at the local County Recorder's Office. This notice includes information about the mortgage, the amount owed, the address of the property, and the date the notice is filed.

The property owner typically has 90 days from the date a "Notice of Default" is filed to make the required payments. The time between the date the default notice is filed and the actual day of sale is called the "publication period." This time period will vary from state to state.

If the loan is not made current or paid in full during the "publication period," the property will be sold at a public auction. The minimum bid is set by the lender as follows:

	Principal loan amount due
+	Applicable late fees
±	<u>Applicable penalties</u>
=	**Minimum bid**

At these auctions, the highest bidder wins. You must be prepared to pay cash on the spot for the foreclosed property. If you can't come up with that kind of money, you'll be especially interested in our next topic, which is . . .

What is an REO?

The initials REO stand for "REAL ESTATE OWNED" property. This term refers to property that was put up for sale at a public foreclosure auction as described above—the catch is, there were no takers. By law, ownership of the property then reverts back to the person or lending institution who made the home loan in the first place. That person or lender is now stuck with the property and will usually want to sell it as fast as possible—and often at unbelievable discount prices! REO values are determined as follows:

	Principal loan amount due
+	Applicable late fees
+	Applicable penalties
±	<u>All costs & fees incurred at the public auction</u>
=	**REO property value (selling price)**

Financing can be arranged for these REO properties, which makes them much easier to buy than properties at a foreclosure auction where you must pay cash. (Unless, of course, you have a money tree growing in the backyard of the home you're now renting!)

How to Find Foreclosures & REOs

Get ready to discover the deals of a lifetime! There are basically five ways to find foreclosures and REOs:

1. Local Lending Institutions

Call ALL the banks and loan companies in your area. Ask to speak with the person who handles foreclosure and REO sales. Ask them how they sell these properties. Tell them what kind of house you are looking for. Be as specific as possible. If they have any properties available, they will usually tell you the location of the property and have you drive by to take a look. If you like what you see, act fast! Call the lender right away and get the ball rolling.

2. Auction Notices Posted at the County Courthouse

Check with the County Recorder or Clerk to find the exact place where notices are posted at your County Courthouse. These notices give you all the relevant information about upcoming foreclosure sales—dates, times, and locations. See the sample on the next page.

3. Public Notices Published in the Newspaper

Lenders are required to give borrowers "sufficient and timely notice" of any foreclosure proceedings against them. This is usually done by printing a public notice in the local newspaper. Default notices are usually published in the Legal Notices section of the paper, but also check the classified ad and real estate sections. These notices give the date, time, and location of upcoming sales.

**YOU ARE IN DEFAULT UNDER A DEED OF TRUST, DATED _____ OCTOBER 16, 1991 _____.
UNLESS YOU TAKE ACTION TO PROTECT YOUR PROPERTY, IT MAY BE SOLD AT A PUBLIC
SALE. IF YOU NEED AN EXPLANATION OF THE NATURE OF THE PROCEEDING AGAINST YOU,
YOU SHOULD CONTACT A LAWYER.**

NOTICE OF TRUSTEE'S SALE

NO. 142220

On NOVEMBER 30, 1994, at 12:00 P.M.
AT THE MAIN ENTRANCE TO THE COUNTY COURTHOUSE,
1100 ANACAPA AVE.

In the city of Santa Barbara, County of Santa Barbara, State of California, CALIFORNIA RECONVEYANCE
COMPANY, a California Corporation, as duly appointed Trustee under that certain Deed of Trust executed by

A SINGLE MAN as trustors,

recorded on OCTOBER 22, 1991, as Instrument No. 91-070639, in Book ---, Page ---, of Official Records of
Santa Barbara County, State of California, under the power of sale therein contained, will sell at public auction to the
highest bidder for cash, or check as described below, payable at the time of sale in lawful money of the United States
of America, without warranty express or implied as to title, use, possession or encumbrances, all right, title and interest
now held by it as such Trustee in and to the following described property situated in the aforesaid County and State,
to wit:
APN: # 121-290-09

PARCEL ONE:
UNIT 9 OF RANCHO GARDENS CONDOMINIUM PLAN, FOR TRACT 5091, IN THE CITY
OF SANTA MARIA, COUNTY OF SANTA BARBARA, STATE OF CALIFORNIA, AS PER
MAP RECORDED IN BOOK 101, PAGES 65 THROUGH 69, INCLUSIVE OF CONDOMINIUMS
IN THE OFFICE OF THE COUNTY RECORDER OF SAID COUNTY.
PARCEL TWO:
AN UNDIVIDED 1/32 INTEREST IN AND TO LOT 33 OF THE CONDOMINIUM PLAN
REFERRED TO IN PARCEL ONE ABOVE.

The total amount of the unpaid principal balance, interest thereon, together with reasonably estimated costs, expenses and
advances at the time of the initial publication of this Notice are ___ $63,336.64 .

Currently dated Cashiers Checks or Certified Checks payable to the Trustee or bidder are acceptable to Trustee provided
proper identification is available.

From information which the Trustee deems reliable, but for which Trustee makes no representation or warranty, the street
address(es) or other common designation of the above described property is:

Said property is being sold for the purpose of paying the obligations secured by said Deed of Trust including fees and
expenses of the Trustee and of Sale.

Dated OCTOBER 20, 1994

CALIFORNIA RECONVEYANCE COMPANY, as said Trustee

By _Suzanne Kelly_ /JH

Suzanne Kelly - Executive Vice President
Address of Trustee:

Chatsworth, California 91311-6519

Telephone Number:

4. Publications Dealing with Financial Matters.

Just about every county in every state has publications that list pending fore-closures. They may be published weekly—or even daily! Sometimes you can subscribe to a service that sends you this information on a regular basis.

How do you find these publications? A good place to start is in the Yellow Pages under headings like Publishers, Newspapers, Financial Data, and Foreclosure Services. Look for companies who publish legal notices from the county recorder's office.

Other places to look are business departments at universities and the county law library. You can also go to your local public library and ask to see the commercial record. This publication lists all the divorces, foreclosures, deaths and probates in your area, and is published for use by attorneys and title companies. Ask around—you may be able to borrow back issues or subscribe to the publication yourself for as little as $8 a month. If you get in the habit of reviewing these records on a regular basis, you'll be "in the know" about foreclosure deals that other people can only dream about!

5. Talk to Everyone You Know.

You can speed up the process of finding a great foreclosure deal by making new friends in the foreclosure industry. As we've said before, making contact with people who buy, sell, and service real estate is probably the best way you can go to uncover these great deals. Don't be shy—keep talking to everyone you meet about what you're looking for.

There are VAST NUMBERS of real estate companies and independent realtors who have made a business of specializing in foreclosure properties. Scan the real estate section of your local newspaper. You'll find their services advertised right and left. Some real estate companies even have 800 numbers that you can call for a pre-recorded list of properties currently being offered. With all these resources to draw on, your search will be so much easier—you never have to feel like you're going it alone!

Like so many things in life, finding a great foreclosure property is a numbers game. You never know where your big break will come from—so keep in mind that you'll reach your goal quicker the more people you talk to about your dream home!

> **Insider's Tip:**
>
> Watch the "For Sale" signs! A couple we met in the course of researching this book had this story to pass onto our readers: "We needed a bigger house for our growing family, and we had our eye on a house just a few miles from where we live now. A For Sale sign had been up for months, and the asking price was just too high for us. But then one day the For Sale sign came down and the house still wasn't sold! Sure enough, we found out that the real estate agent hadn't been able to sell the house, and the owners were desperate. We went to them directly and were able to buy our new house for a song!"

Move Fast for Best Results

Once you've identified the property you're interested in, it's back to the drawing board—the research drawing board, that is! Always remember that when you are trying to purchase foreclosures or REOs, time is of the essence, so move quickly! This next layer of your research is very important, and since foreclosure properties are usually sold quickly, you don't have a lot of time to seek out the following important information:

Liens, Liens, Who's Got the Liens?

Visit your local Hall of Records or County Recorder's Office and look up the property you are interested in. Find out if there are any mechanic's or tax liens against the property. If so, the people who hold those liens will be first in line to bid on it.

There's another benefit to finding out about those liens—you'll save yourself a lot of time if you discover the outstanding liens are so high you can't purchase the property at an affordable price.

> **Insider's Tip:**
>
> Pay the lienholder a visit yourself, and try to make a deal with them privately before the auction! This is a great strategy that REALLY WORKS!

Easements, Appraisals and Other Surprises

Visit your County Assessor's Office and ask for a copy of the parcel map and the most recent appraisal of the property you are interested in. You'll learn a great deal by carefully reviewing these documents.

Compare the appraised value with the amount you can pay for the property. Remember, only YOU can decide what the property is really worth to you, and the appraised value may help you make this decision!

Look for any "easements" on the property. These are permissions granted for use of certain areas of the property by the county, city, state or federal government. For example, sometimes the city or county might claim the right of access to your property to make improvements to the sewer system. Some easements may even restrict the ways you can use your own property! Ask the Assessor's Office for help in determining how any easements will affect your ownership.

A thorough review of the parcel map will also show correct property lines and other things to look for when you visit the property.

Inspect the Property

The next step is to get yourself over to the property. Walk around and over it with a pencil, paper, and a sharp eye. If you know a good building contractor, it'll be worth your while to bring him/her along to inspect the property with you. Your contractor friend will know exactly what to look for in terms of potential repairs, like cracks in the foundation, signs of termites, heating duct replacements, etc.

Inspecting a home can be dirty work . . . but climbing up into attics and under the house can reveal many things that you as a potential homeowner will want to know before you make a bid. Please refer to Chapter 18 and take our handy-dandy home inspection checklist with you when you visit the property.

Attending An Auction

Once you're confident you've collected enough information to bid on the property of your choice, you're ALMOST ready to attend the auction. There's one more step you can take to improve your chances of making the winning bid. If there are other auctions going on in your area, try to attend a few just to familiarize yourself with the process. Watch what goes on, and afterwards go up to the people you saw bidding and ask them questions.

It's also a good idea to re-contact the people who have helped you so far in your research and ask them to pass along any tips they may have from their experience in attending auctions. Most of these people will be only too happy to pass on their knowledge to you!

Making an offer on property through a Realtor is very different from bidding at an auction. You may find yourself bidding against experienced investors who have made fortunes in the foreclosure game. You may also be bidding against first-time homebuyers or even disgruntled relatives!

The old saying "knowledge is power" definitely applies here. Attending a few auctions will stack the odds in your favor and help you place the winning bid!

Rules of REO Sales

As we mentioned earlier in this chapter, properties that are not sold at public auction become the property of the bank or lender and are then known as REOs. When this happens, the rules of the game change a little as well.

The good news is that you can often arrange financing on these properties. The lender who owns the REO is the first place to begin. Chances are you'll already have talked to the lender from the research you've done on the property, so most of your energy can now be concentrated on arranging financing and beating out the competition—if there is any!

Ask the lender to give you a specific overview of the steps that will be necessary for you to purchase the REO property. In general, here's what you'll have to look forward to:

1. Inspecting the property
2. Arranging financing
3. Making an offer (see next page)

Enlist the help of the lender in preparing your offer. Remember, it is usually in their best interest to sell the REO property as quickly as possible—after all, they are really in the money business, not the real estate business. You'll find a good working relationship with the lender will save you time and money—in fact, it's worth its weight in gold! It's easy to establish this kind of relationship—just use common courtesy and politeness. By now you know what you want—and you're practically in the door!

Sample Offer Letter to a Bank for an REO Property

DATE

BANK NAME
BANK ADDRESS
ATTN: CONTACT NAME
REAL ESTATE REO/TRUST SALES DEPARTMENT

RE: PROPERTY ID #
        PROPERTY ADDRESS

Dear_____:

As previously discussed, please accept this letter as an offer
on the property located at_____:

PURCHASE PRICE:
DOWN PAYMENT:
FINANCING TERMS:
CLOSING DATE:

AMOUNT ENCLOSED (deposit/binder):

Please contact me as follows with your acceptance:

        Your Name
        Your Address
        Your Telephone Number (day & eve)

                      Thank you very much.

                      Your signature

Insider's Tip:

In the course of our research, we learned about a case where the buyer's persistence really paid off.

This buyer made it a habit to read the "notices of default" published in the local newspaper, and through these notices she discovered a well maintained 3-bedroom, 2-bath house in a good neighborhood. She did her research and was ready to attend the auction and make her bid on the house.

Then, the date of the auction was postponed—not once, not twice, but three times! By the time the auction finally took place, our friend was the only bidder who showed up—and the starting bid had been reduced by $20,000!

Needless to say, our friend is now the proud owner of a beautiful home—and for a price that would make the neighbors green with envy if they knew about it!

Bankruptcy Sales

Another way to purchase foreclosure properties is through bankruptcy sales. These sales occur when a person or a business needs to liquidate all their assets to pay off their debts. To find properties being sold in this way, you must first contact the court-appointed trustee that handles these cases for your area. They will explain their process of accepting verbal or written bids on property they must liquidate.

Here is a simple three-step guide to get you started:

1. Go to Appendix B in this book, "Area Trustees for Bankruptcy Sales." Locate the area you are interested in and call the Trustee for that region. Ask them for a list of the trustees in your specific town or city. Most likely they will ask you to come to their office and pick up the list, or send them a business-sized self-addressed, stamped envelope and a note requesting it.

2. Once you receive the list, contact the local trustee and explain to them the kind of property you are looking for. Most trustees will put your name on a mailing list to be notified when they have bankruptcy property for sale.

3. Once a property becomes available, you'll need to follow local procedures for placing a bid. The local Trustee will let you know how to do this. Bankruptcy sales follow a similar procedure to REO sales explained above.

Also, don't forget your trusty local newspaper! The classified real estate ads often have notices of bank liquidations, like the one shown below. Bankruptcy sales are another potential gold mine for you, the buyer in search of discount real estate. So, use the contacts listed below and the information included in this chapter, and you'll soon be on your way to home ownership at prices you never believed possible!

Chapter 7: Delinquent Tax Sales

Now let's look at another area of great opportunities to find yourself a discount home—delinquent tax sales! Properties with unpaid federal, state, or property taxes are sold very much like properties with unpaid mortgages (See Chapter 6, Bank Foreclosures and REOs). The main difference is that property owners usually have a longer time to clear up tax debt than to pay past due mortgages with banks or other lenders. Usually several warnings are sent, and the taxpayer is given a period of time to resolve the balance. If that doesn't get results, the property is eventually sold at a public auction.

It's possible for buyers like yourself to get INCREDIBLE DEALS at these delinquent tax sales. Auction procedures for federal and state tax foreclosures vary from state to state. Some hold a sale every other month, some have a sale every other year, and some sell properties only as they become available. Since each county has a slightly different approach to selling tax delinquent properties, you'll need to do some local legwork before attending a public auction.

The Fast Track to Bargains

Here's a simple step-by-step method you can use to find out about tax-delinquent properties in your area:

1. Check your local newspaper regularly or visit the County Courthouse to find listings of tax delinquent sales.

2. You can also call direct. Look in your telephone book under County Government, and find a department title like County Tax Collector, Assessor, Treasurer, Clerk, or Property Redemption. When you call these offices, ask them very specific questions about tax-delinquent property for sale in your area, such as:

• "When homeowners are delinquent in paying their property taxes, when and how do you go about selling the properties?

• "Are there any properties available now?"

• "How and when do you advertise the sale of these properties?"

• "Could you please add my name to your mailing list so that I will be notified of any upcoming sales?"

These phone calls might get you a list of properties which will be auctioned soon, along with legal descriptions of the parcels, assessed value, and minimum opening bid information. Or, you may find out that the properties are sold through individual brokers. If this is the case, ask which ones, write down the names, then call the brokers.

Sometimes it takes a little perseverance, but eventually you will get the information that can lead you to your bargain home! Just remember that in the search for your dream home, you must leave "no stone unturned."

Insider's Tip:

Some counties may not do anything about a tax delinquent property unless someone comes up to them and inquires about buying it. If this is the case in your area, go to the County Courthouse and ask to see the deeds of properties which are delinquent. Then proceed as described below.

---

3. Learn to Read the Legal Descriptions. These will tell you the exact location of the property within an established grid pattern for your area. When looking at a legal description, you may see something like: "North 0°22'6" West . . . etc." At first, this may look a little confusing—but if you ask someone at the County Records Office to help you read the legal descriptions, you'll soon become familiar with them. (You'll be amazed at what asking a simple question can reveal! Also, you're likely to be impressed with how cooperative and friendly most people are.)

Through this process you'll learn about the development history of the property you want to buy, as well as the history of the surrounding area. This information will be VERY IMPORTANT to you in deciding whether to buy the property or not.

Visit the Property

Once you have found some properties which interest you, go out and visit them in person. Remember that these properties are usually sold far below market value, and they are sold with <u>no guarantees</u> about the condition, zoning, title or anything else. To take full advantage of a tax delinquent sale, it's best to do another layer of research to check out the following things before putting your money down at the auction.

Again, the people at your County Records Office are a good resource for this kind of information—they are usually very willing to help. So be courteous, ask your questions, and you'll be richly rewarded for your efforts!

1. Tax Liens and Mechanics Liens
Find out if there are any tax liens or mechanics liens on the property. Ideally you'll find a property free and clear of these liens, but if there are small amounts due you may be able to pay them off and still get the property for a bargain price.

2. Fair Market Value

If you like the property's location and you're ready to buy, first check with the County Tax Assessor's Office and find out how much similar properties have sold for recently. This will help you determine the fair market value of the property you're interested in.

3. Maximum Bid Price

Set a maximum bid price in your mind. This is a personal decision. Decide what price would mean that the property is a really good buy for you. Once you've established this price, promise yourself that you won't go beyond it. Don't get caught up in the excitement of the auction and pay too much.

There's another strategy you can try before the auction. Go to see the property owner in person and ask if you can come to an agreement. He or she may say no, but on the other hand, the owner may be anxious to sell the property and clear up the tax debt as soon as possible. If this is the case, you have the clear advantage of purchasing the property before there's any competition!

At the Auction

If you can't make a purchase prior to auction day, you'll need to attend the auction itself. You may or may not find other people bidding against you—so be prepared!

Bring your money with you—either cash, travelers checks, a certified check, cashiers check, or a money order made out for the maximum amount you are going to bid. Don't worry—if you win with a lesser bid, they will give you a refund!

The opening bid is either a set percentage of the property's value, OR an amount which would cover the fees involved in the sale. <u>If you're the only person there, you need only offer the minimum bid and the property is yours!</u>

Usually a "transfer tax" and recording fee are added to the winning bid. The recording fee is often relatively low, but the transfer tax may equal 6% of the assessed value of the property or more.

Don't expect to receive your deed right away, because the sale must be confirmed by the court. It could take four months or longer after a tax sale to finalize the deal. Also, you'll be responsible for obtaining a title search before you can get a mortgage from a lender. But believe us, these are small tasks compared to the great thrill of finding these homes for low, low prices!

Wake Up and Smell the Tax Sales!

In the meantime, don't ever lose heart! You won't be sorry you took the time to find discounts like these. Be careful and do your research. Keep asking lots of questions, with your ears and eyes open and your notepad ready. You could be one of the lucky people who buys a tax delinquent home for a fraction of its real value—and uses the extra money to make some of your OTHER dreams come true!

Chapter 8:
Probate and Estate Sales

Whoever said "You can't take it with you" was certainly right when it comes to real estate. Houses often become available for pur chase at bargain prices after an individual's death—especially if the heirs live out-of-state, if there is no will, or if the will is contested and the property ends up being owned by the city or county government.

The sources you can investigate to learn about probate sales in your area are described below. Probate sales are common in just about every area of the country—and it's simple to find out about these fantastic deals. Just follow the steps outlined here, and you'll have another great source of discount properties at your service!

Probate Department or Surrogate Court

Look up the Probate Department under Surrogate Court in your phone book under local city or county government offices. Give them a call and ask them how they sell real estate property obtained through probate in your area.

In some locations, you'll be able to get this information quickly and easily; in other places, you may have to talk to several people before you find the answer to this question. Different cities and counties across the nation have different procedures for disposing of properties through probate. Get to know the procedure that applies to your specific area, and you'll be ready for action when the time is right!

Read the Commercial Record

Your friendly public library has copies of the commercial record, a publication which lists all the deaths and probates in your area. If you're serious about finding houses via probate, you'll benefit greatly from getting to know this publication. By reading it regularly, you'll gain inside information that you can use to get a jump on the best opportunities in probate and estate sales in your area.

Read the Classifieds

The real estate section of the classifieds is a great place to find deals on probate and estate sales. A couple of sample ads are shown below.

ESTATE SALE
Priced/for sale this weekend. 3 Br 2 Ba. dbl wide in beautiful East Mission Valley Senior Park. Superb end lot. Clean & ready for immediate move-in. Only $6,800.

PROBATE SALE
3 br. 2 ba. sold as is. L.G. schools. Prvt street, court overbid. $215,855. Call today!

Read the Obituaries

Although this might sound dreary, it's a surefire way of finding out if the deceased person has heirs who live out-of-state. If this is the case, they may want to liquidate the property for a number of reasons—the main reason being that they live too far away to maintain or manage the property. To investigate further, you must find out who is the executor of the estate. A trip to the County Clerk's Office for a copy of the death certificate will help, because then you can contact the person listed as "Informant" on the certificate for more information.

Don't Judge a Book by Its Cover!

In many cases, probate properties aren't much to look at. If an elderly person has spent the past 30 years living alone in their house, you can bet that the paint is peeling, the back step is broken, and the landscaping is neglected.

Should these things discourage you? Absolutely not! In fact, you WANT to find properties in this condition, since cosmetic problems like this often discourage other buyers and leave the door wide open for YOU to pick up a house for an incredibly low price!

Painting, landscaping, and repairs to things like broken steps are easy to fix, especially if you can do some of the work yourself. All you need to do is make a complete list of the needed repairs. Then get cost estimates for the bigger jobs you can't tackle on your own. As long as the cost of buying the house plus the cost of repairs doesn't exceed the price you could sell the house for once it's fixed up, you're home free!

What Happens During a Probate or Estate Sale

While procedures vary from city to city and state to state, chances are that the path you'll follow to buy a property through a probate or estate sale will look something like this:

• When an estate goes through probate as a result of the deceased person leaving no will or some other extenuating circumstance, the house will be auctioned off.

• When the auction date has been set, the Probate Department prepares a report called: "Report and Confirmation of Sale of Real Property."

• This report is usually available two weeks before the court date. If you find a house you want, you have to act fast. Do the same kind of research on the house as outlined in Chapter 6, Bank Foreclosures and REOs.

• Contact the executor of the estate, and see if you can make an offer before the property is auctioned. If you can't, be sure to attend the court hearing listed on the "Report and Confirmation of Sale of Real Property" notice—and be sure to get there on time, because the bidding starts right away!

• Once the minimum bid is opened, the judge calls for any "over bids" from the public. This is your chance! The property will be sold to the highest bidder. At many auctions, there are very few bidders—you might even find that you're the only one who shows up to bid on the property!

Can You Swing a Private Sale?

The best deals can be found when the terms of the will allow a private sale. You must contact the executor of the estate and ask if this is possible. The permission of the court may not be required—and if it isn't, you can jump right in, inspect the property quickly, and make an offer!

Most states have a waiting period of 30 to 60 days before the deal can be completed. The purpose of the waiting period is to allow for higher bids or written objections to be filed. Your bid should be fine as long as it's within 10 percent of the executor's appraisal.

Probate and estate sales require extra patience and attention to detail. The courts have built plenty of protection into the process of buying a house under these conditions. Allow extra time for the unforeseen delays, and you'll be rewarded with a prize that's well worth waiting for!

Proceed with Caution!

In doing our research for this chapter, we encountered much advice about the need to be cautious when investigating probate and estate sales. The executor of the estate and the estate's heirs are likely to be very sensitive just after the death of their loved one. Feelings are often unpredictable, and people can feel very vulnerable at a time like this.

It's a good time to use the Golden Rule—be respectful of people's feelings at all times, and treat them as you would wish to be treated. Depending on your own feelings, you may feel comfortable investigating probate sales only if you know the people involved or are familiar with the property through other personal or business connections.

When we investigated probate sales for this book, we discovered that the people who had succeeded at these deals were extra patient and took the time to make sure all the details of the sale were just so. One fellow was able to purchase the home of his best friend's parents. His friend lived out of state and was not interested in buying the property. It helped that the buyer wasn't in any hurry to move. As described above, the approval process took awhile. But at the end, this man got an especially good deal, and he is now happily living in a roomy house with a view!

So use your head, follow up on the leads you discover, and allow enough time for the deal to close—and you too could join the ranks of VERY satisfied homebuyers from probate and estate sales!

Chapter 9:
IRS Sales

When people don't pay their federal income taxes, or if they fail to honestly report their earnings, the IRS doesn't hesitate to step in and liquidate their real estate assets immediately! All property seized in this manner is sold "as is"—but if you find an IRS property you're interested in, you're allowed to have it inspected before the sale. And that's a good thing—our research has shown that when it comes to sales like this, an inspection is absolutely necessary!

IRS sales and auctions follow the same regulations nationwide. They are generally conducted in the very same local district where the seizure was made. But each sale is different. Some houses are better deals than others. What makes some deals better than others depends on how much is owed in back taxes, and how much the property would be worth on the market today.

The bottom line is that no property can sell for less than what is owed to the IRS. <u>There is truly unbelievable potential for great deals here!</u> Payment is generally due at the time of sale. If your bid buys the property, you will receive a tax receipt after six months, which you then turn in for a tax deed—and the property is yours.

Do a Title Search

The IRS doesn't guarantee clear title to any home purchased at an IRS sale. This means that YOU must do a title search on any property you're interested in. It's smart to do this before you place your bid, because there may be liens against the property which you would assume at the time of purchase. You could end up paying off all the debts of the previous owner! Or worse, you could lose the property to one of the lienholders!

Department of the T   sury / Internal Revenue Service

Notice of

Public Auction Sale

Under the authority in Internal Revenue Code section 6331, the property described below has been seized for nonpayment of internal revenue taxes due from

_____

The property will be sold at public auction as provided by Internal Revenue Code section 6335 and related regulations.

Date of Sale: _____December 21,_____ 19 _94_

Time of Sale: _____10:00_____ am -XXX

Place of Sale: Internal Revenue Service Lobby

Title Offered: Only the right, title, and interest of
in and to the property will be offered for sale. If requested, the Internal Revenue Service will furnish information about possible encumbrances, which may be useful in determining the value of the interest being sold (See the back of this form for further details.)

Description of Property:
Assessors Parcel Number 079-060-50
Real Property in the unincorporated area of the County of Santa Barbara, State of California, described as:

Government Lot 2 and the West half of the Southeast quarter of the northwest quarter of Section 30, Township 5 North, Range 29 West, San Bernardino Base and Meridian in the County of Santa Barbara, State of California, containing approximately 28.15 acres more or less.

The East ½ of the Southeast ½ of the Northwest ½ of Section 30, Township 5 North, Range 29 West, San Bernardino Base and Meridian, in the County of Santa Barbara, State of California.

TOGETHER WITH an undivided 20/96ths water rights as set out in Agreement dated April 12, 1971, recorded April 15, 1971 as Instrument number 10739, Book 2343, Page 1281 in the office of the county recorder of said county.

Government Lot 1 of Section 30, Township 5 North, Range 29 West, San Bernardino Base and Meridian, in the County of Santa Barbara, State of California.

TOGETHER WITH an undivided 8/96ths water rights as set out in Agreement dated April 12, 1971, recorded April 15, 1971 as Instrument number 10739, Book 2343, Page 1281 in the office of the county recorder of said county.

Property may be Inspected at: By appointment. Contact_____ Revenue Officer for appointment.

Payment Terms:
☐ Full payment required on acceptance of highest bid
☒ Deferred payment as follows: 20% of purchase price upon acceptance of highest bid with balance to be paid no later than one week after the sale.

Form of Payment: All payments must be by cash, certified check, cashier's or treasurer's check or by a United States postal, bank, express, or telegraph money order. Make check or money order payable to the Internal Revenue Service.

Signature	Name and Title *(Typed)*	Date
Address for information About the Sale Internal Revenue Service		Phone

Form **2434** (Rev. 3-84)

No matter how much you want the property, it's best to let it go if you find title problems. We learned about a buyer who wanted a particular house so badly that he went ahead with the sale anyway, even though the title wasn't crystal-clear. He ended up having to go into foreclosure himself shortly after he moved into the house because he couldn't pay the previous owner's debts—not a pretty picture! Don't let the same thing happen to you!

Buyer Beware: The 6-Month Redemption Period

All real estate disposed of at IRS sales and auctions has a six-month redemption period—which means that the original owner, or any interested party with a claim, has the right to buy the property back by paying you the purchase price plus 20% interest per annum. In reality, this rarely happens—but it's something you should know and keep in mind when you weigh the pros and cons of buying an IRS property. And it's all the more reason to do a title search as described above!

Where to Find IRS Sales

To find out about IRS sales in your area, you have four options:

1. Watch your local newspapers under AUCTION NOTICES & CLASSIFIEDS.

2. Look for IRS AUCTION NOTICES which are placed in local Post Offices or your County Courthouse. See the sample notice on the opposite page.

3. Call EG&G Dynatrend at 703/351-7887. This company conducts public sales of seized property for the U.S. Customs Service. Sometimes they dispose of real estate that was seized by the IRS. They will send you a schedule of upcoming auctions plus information on how to participate. These auctions are held approximately every nine weeks in Texas, New Jersey, Florida, California, and Arizona. See the sample schedule on the next page!

4) Contact the IRS directly at one of its offices. You will find a complete list in Appendix C of this book!

Insider's Tip:

Stay in touch with the IRS office right up to the day of the sale. You may suddenly find the sale is canceled if the homeowner is somehow able to settle the IRS's claim. A telephone call at the last minute can save you much wasted time and effort!

IRS Offices

The list of IRS offices in Appendix C is broken down into the seven IRS regions. Each office handles its own sales and is not required to inform any other office or consult them. You can call or write them directly. If you wish to be placed on the "bidder's list," indicate the exact geographic area you are interested in and the fact that you are interested in real property (homes, hotels, land, farms, etc).

Send the letter to the appropriate address and mark it to the attention of SPECIAL PROCEDURES. Then, just sit back and wait for these great opportunities to be delivered to your doorstep. Remember, someone has to take advantage of these amazing deals—and it might as well be you!

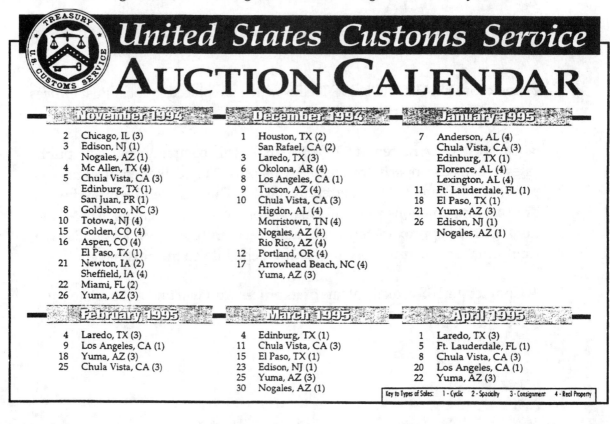

United States Customs Service
AUCTION CALENDAR

November 1994		December 1994		January 1995	
2	Chicago, IL (3)	1	Houston, TX (2)	7	Anderson, AL (4)
3	Edison, NJ (1)		San Rafael, CA (2)		Chula Vista, CA (3)
	Nogales, AZ (1)	3	Laredo, TX (3)		Edinburg, TX (1)
4	Mc Allen, TX (4)	6	Okolona, AR (4)		Florence, AL (4)
5	Chula Vista, CA (3)	8	Los Angeles, CA (1)		Lexington, AL (4)
	Edinburg, TX (1)	9	Tucson, AZ (4)	11	Ft. Lauderdale, FL (1)
	San Juan, PR (1)	10	Chula Vista, CA (3)	18	El Paso, TX (1)
8	Goldsboro, NC (3)		Higdon, AL (4)	21	Yuma, AZ (3)
10	Totowa, NJ (4)		Morristown, TN (4)	26	Edison, NJ (1)
15	Golden, CO (4)		Nogales, AZ (4)		Nogales, AZ (1)
16	Aspen, CO (4)		Rio Rico, AZ (4)		
	El Paso, TX (1)	12	Portland, OR (4)		
21	Newton, IA (2)	17	Arrowhead Beach, NC (4)		
	Sheffield, IA (4)		Yuma, AZ (3)		
22	Miami, FL (2)				
26	Yuma, AZ (3)				

February 1995		March 1995		April 1995	
4	Laredo, TX (3)	4	Edinburg, TX (1)	1	Laredo, TX (3)
9	Los Angeles, CA (1)	11	Chula Vista, CA (3)	5	Ft. Lauderdale, FL (1)
18	Yuma, AZ (3)	15	El Paso, TX (1)	8	Chula Vista, CA (3)
25	Chula Vista, CA (3)	23	Edison, NJ (1)	20	Los Angeles, CA (1)
		25	Yuma, AZ (3)	22	Yuma, AZ (3)
		30	Nogales, AZ (1)		

Key to Types of Sales: 1 - Cyclic   2 - Specialty   3 - Consignment   4 - Real Property

Chapter 10 :
GSA Sales

Have you ever heard of buying surplus property from Uncle Sam? If you haven't, you're not alone! The General Services Administration (GSA) is a Federal agency that's a well-kept secret to most people. The GSA operates the Federal Property Resource Service (FPRS) to sell surplus Federal property to the general public—meaning, to folks just like you and me!

In effect, the GSA operates as the real estate agency for the Federal Government. The GSA's real estate professionals market property in all 50 states, the District of Columbia, Puerto Rico, the Virgin Islands, and the U.S. Pacific territories. All sorts of property that's no longer needed by the Feds is up for sale—from lighthouses to missile sites, and from industrial and agricultural properties to single family houses and vacant lots.

Needless to say, you've got an incredible variety of properties to choose from—and the prices are even more incredible! Don't let these deals pass you by—use the information here to make a deal that can't be beat!

Where to Go, What to Do

There are several ways to find out about properties that are on the market RIGHT NOW through the GSA. First, you can write or call the GSA for a booklet called the "U.S. Real Property Sales List" at this address:

> Properties
> Consumer Information Center
> Pueblo, Colorado 81009
> (617) 565 - 5700

This booklet, which comes out quarterly, includes listings for all 50 states. Even better, it contains two forms for you to fill out. The first form puts you on the mailing list so you'll receive future issues of the U.S. Real Property Sales List. The second form signs you up to receive notices about particular types of properties. On this form, you can specify the properties you're interested in by state, by type (agricultural, commercial, industrial, or residential), and by how much you're willing to spend. You'll then receive a flyer mailed to your home address with the properties that match your description.

GSA Regional and Field Offices

You can also obtain a copy of the U.S. Real Property Sales List by calling or writing one of the regional or field offices listed below.

GSA Regional Offices

Region 1
(Connecticut, Maine, Massachusetts, New Hampshire, New York, New Jersey, Illinois, Indiana, Michigan, Ohio, Wisconsin, Rhode Island)
Office of Real Estate Sales
U.S. General Services Administration
10 Causeway Street
Boston, MA 02222
(617) 565-5700

Region 4
(Puerto Rico, Virgin Islands, Delaware, Florida, Georgia, Kentucky, Washington, D.C., Maryland, Mississippi, Virginia, West Virginia, Alabama, Pennsylvania, North Carolina, South Carolina, Tennessee)
Office of Real Estate Sales
U.S. General Services Administration
Peachtree Summit Building
401 West Peachtree Street
Atlanta, GA 30365-2550
(404) 331-5133

Region 7
(Colorado, Minnesota, North Dakota, Utah, Wyoming, Iowa,
Kansas, Missouri, Nebraska, Arkansas, Louisiana, New Mexico,
Texas, Montana, Oklahoma, South Dakota)
Office of Real Estate Sales
U.S. General Services Administration
819 Taylor Street
Fort Worth, TX 76102
(817) 334 - 2331

Region 9
(Arizona, California, Hawaii, Nevada, American Samoa,
Guam, the Trust Territory of the Pacific Islands, Alaska, Oregon,
Idaho, Washington)
Office of Real Estate Sales
U.S. General Services Administration
525 Market Street
San Francisco, CA 94105
(415) 744 - 5952

GSA Field Offices

Office of Real Estate Sales
U.S. General Services Administration
230 South Dearborn St., Rm. 3864
Chicago, IL 60604
(312) 353 - 6045

Office of Real Estate Sales
U.S. General Services Administration
400 15th St. SW, Room 1138
Auburn, WA 98001
(206) 931 - 7547

OK, I've Got the Sales List—Now What?

If you're interested in a property on the sales list, your next step is to call the phone number included with the list and request a bid package. The phone number will connect you with the GSA regional or field office that's handling the sale.

The bid package will include photos of the property, plus the terms and conditions of the sale. Large properties are generally sold at auction, and smaller, less expensive properties are sold by sealed bid. You must place a bid deposit and make your offer on a special bidding form. All the bids are opened on a specified date, and the property goes to the highest bidder.

How to Find the Best Deals

Most sales of the GSA are for cash only—but there ARE exceptions. If the value of a property is judged too low to be worth marketing through the U.S. Real Property Sales List, the GSA can sell it by advertising in local newspapers—or even in publications like the *Wall Street Journal* and *USA Today*.

> ### Insider's Tip:
>
> The GSA runs frequent ads in *USA Today*. So do not hesitate to call direct to the regional or field offices of the GSA and ask about upcoming properties that will be advertised in the newspaper!

The Electronic Bulletin Board

If you have a computer with a modem, you can take advantage of the latest in modern technology to go on line with the Federal Real Estate Sales Electronic Bulletin Board.

This computer bulletin board is a great source of additional information about properties being offered by the GSA. You'll find more detailed information here than in the U.S. Real Property Sales List—and there are also MORE properties listed on the computer than in the printed version!

All you do is dial **1-800-776-7872,** and you'll be connected to the bulletin board without charge! From the Washington, D.C. metropolitan area, dial (202) 501-6510. Set your computer communications software to 8 data bits, no parity, and 1 stop bit, and you'll be ready to go!

RESIDENTIAL PROPERTIES*

Location and Description of Properties

PARCEL 1A

Located on 9.39-acres, this unfinished 2,160 sq. ft. residence features three bedrooms and two baths. The living room is highlighted by a large fireplace. A deck surrounds the house and offers great views of the mountains. The 2,160 sq. ft. basement is used as a garage and for storage.

ASSESSOR'S PARCEL NO.:
3350-006-900
ZONING:
LAC11 – Single Residential

Bid Deposit Required:
$5,000.00

PARCEL 2A

This 1,605 sq. ft. ranch style home contains three bedrooms, two baths and a family room with fireplace. Located on a 9,240 sq. ft. lot in a quiet well-tended neighborhood, this comfortable home also provides a large family-style kitchen, natural wood closets and a covered front porch and rear patio. An attached two-car garage completes the home.

ASSESSOR'S PARCEL NO.:	**2688-006-013**
ZONING:	**R-1 SFR**
Bid Deposit Required:	**$5,000.00**

*All residences are vacant.

Separate bid deposits are required for each property.
All properties subject to sale or withdrawal without prior notice.

Success Secrets

As of 1994, there were 13,000 people in California alone on the U.S. Real Property mailing list. This means that the word is getting out, AND that there are plenty of good deals to be made!

Timing is everything when you want to find and bid on a GSA property. For best results, once you receive your copy of the U.S. Real Property Sales List, you must follow through QUICKLY and request your bid packages right away. Also, don't forget to call the regional or field offices of the GSA often to ask about properties being sold via newspaper advertising.

The GSA is known to offer some real gems—as well as offbeat properties you won't find anywhere else. We know a middle-aged couple who wanted to leave the big-city rat race and find a simpler lifestyle on the coast. Through the GSA, they found a lighthouse that was just perfect for them. Now they spend their days doing something they really enjoy in a setting close to nature.

No matter what your dream is, chances are the GSA has a property that will pique your interest—and maybe even one that will make your dream come true!

Chapter 11:
VA Repossessions

Veterans Administration repossessions happen when homes that used to have VA guaranteed loans go into foreclosure. Afterwards, these homes are owned by the VA and must be sold off.

You'll find all kinds of homes to choose from—from single-family houses to duplexes, triplexes, and fourplexes, not to mention condominiums and townhouses. And the price is right—you can often buy VA repos discounted to as much as 25% below their appraised value!

What If You're Not a Veteran?

Good news! The great thing about VA repos is that you DON'T have to be a veteran to buy a VA repo or to assume a VA loan. We know both veterans and non-veterans who've had outstanding success in obtaining discount homes through the VA. So don't delay, get out there and take advantage of these great deals NOW!

How to Find VA Repos

Many VA repos are listed with real estate brokers and the multiple listing service. Realtors will be more than happy to show you the properties that best meet your needs.

If you'd rather go it on your own, you'll be amazed at how easy it is to locate VA repos. Call one of the VA offices listed in Appendix D at the back of this book. Most offices have telephone recordings with the latest properties. Some even have special computer bulletin boards with VA property listings that you can access if you have a computer and modem at your home or office. These numbers are all listed in Appendix D.

But probably the easiest way to find VA repos is to check the classified section of your nearest big city newspaper. In Los Angeles, for example, VA properties are listed in the classified real estate section of the *LA Times* on the first and third Fridays of every month. Along with the listings of actual properties, the newspaper also includes complete instructions on how to place a bid. See the next two pages for an example.

Call the classified ad department of your nearest metropolitan newspaper and ask them if they list VA properties on special days. It won't be long before you've found a house you want to own—and then it's time to place your bid!

Placing a Bid

The process of bidding on a VA repo goes like this:

• With VA properties, the understanding is that all sales are "as is." That means you must check out the property as thoroughly as possible before you place your bid. Sometimes the listing will say that plumbing, heating, and electrical repairs will be made after closing—in which case you can rest assured that those systems will be working when you move in.

• After your inspection, submit your bid on the property through a real estate agent or broker. The VA will pay their fee, so don't worry about losing any money out of pocket! The bid must be submitted on a special VA contract form. All bids are sealed, and you must bid at least the minimum amount on the sales sheet.

Insider's Tip:

Bid an unusual amount to increase your odds of winning—for example, $40,001.99 instead of $40,000.

• The three highest bids are submitted to the State VA Office, where a Loan Examiner investigates each bid received and then qualifies the buyer. This means that you, as the buyer, must meet the VA's approval before they let you assume the mortgage. If you've gotten this far, you have an excellent

HOMES FOR SALE
U.S. Department of Veterans Affairs

Available to Veterans and non-Veterans. 8.5% (apr 8.75%) interest rate, effective June 1, on term financing now available. To inspect a property and/or submit an offer see any broker.

CLOSING DATE: 4:00 P.M. October 11, 1994

PM NO.	PRICE	MIN. DOWN PMT.	SQ. FT.	BED/ BATH	STATUS
1. 76150	$25,000	0%	1002	2/1	TLBO-TM
2. 2003092	$20,000	0%	1004	2/1	TLBFO-TM*
3. 2136432	$125,000	0%	857	2/1	AL
4. 66706	$54,000	CASH ONLY	840	3/1	CLB*
5. 2102569	$112,000	0%	1133	3/2	AL-TM
6. 1989512	$66,000	0%	1036	3/1	TLB*
7. 1980926	$63,000	0%	1272	2/2	TLB-TM
8. 2002988	$105,000	0%	1710	4/3	TLB-TM
9. 2023329	$83,000	0%	1429	3/3	TLBO-TM
10. 2004367	$91,000	0%	1008	3/2	AL
11. 2049081	$95,000	0%	1070	2/2	AL-TM
12. 1999045	$140,000	0%	1263	3/2	TLB-TM*
13. 2054938	$101,000	0%	1975	3/2	AL-TM
14. 2077018	$96,000	0%	1654	3/3	AL-TM
15. 2064855	$82,000	0%	1397	3/2	AL-TM
16. 2113272	$102,000	0%	1637	3/2	AL-TM
17. 2065372	$150,000	0%	1215	2/3	AL-TM
18. 2024817	$110,000	0%	1320	3/2	TLB-TM
19. 2081088	$25,000	0%	765	1/2	TLBOF-TM
20. 2001833	$65,000	0%	758	2/1	AL-TM
21. 2048929	$65,000	0%	779	2/1	AL-TM
22. 1760613	$80,000	0%	958	2/2	AL-TM
23. 1964411	$100,000	0%	985	2/1	TLB
24. 2069323	$90,000	0%	1050	3/1	TLB-TM*
25. 2090477	$38,000	0%	418	0/1	AL-TM
26. 2040664	$50,000	0%	758	2/2	TLB-TM
27. 2018787	$110,000	0%	1400	3/1	TLBF
28. 2004627	$100,000	0%	838	2/1	TLB-TM*
29. 1722588	$39,000	0%	1344	3/2	TLB-TM
30. 1731555	$102,000	0%	2196	4/3	AL
31. 2077900	$76,000	0%	1309	3/2	AL
32. 2036138	$90,000	0%	1508	3/2	AL
33. 1734548	$82,000	0%	1474	3/3	AL
34. 2035755	$75,000	0%	1284	3/2	AL
35. 2059022	$110,000	0%	1117	3/2	AL
36. 2134656	$120,000	0%	1460	3/2	TLBF-TM
37. 1969827	$79,000	0%	1278	4/2	TLBF-TM*
38. 2068497	$73,000	0%	1014	2/2	TLB-TM
39. 2021197	$59,000	0%	915	3/1	TLB-TM
40. 1766893	$74,000	0%	1035	2/2	AL-TM
41. 1922345	$122,000	0%	1524	4/2	TLB-TM
42. 1767896	$49,000	0%	1136	3/2	TLBFO-TM*
43. 1972933	$44,000	0%	1132	3/1	TLBOF-TM*
44. 1893007	$74,000	0%	902	3/1	TLBF-TM*
45. 2081499	$96,500	0%	1437	4/2	TLB*
46. 2102024	$109,000	10%	1262	4/2	AL
47. 2055880	$81,000	0%	1578	4/2	TLB*
48. 2027976	$96,000	0%	1248	3/2	TLB*

For Properties on which we did not receive any bids, late offers will be accepted through the Friday following the closing date.

Status codes: (A) Property is eligible for VA/FHA, conventional financing, all cash or term offers. On FHA financing, buyers lender orders appraisal. On VA guaranteed financing, VA will issue CRV. **(B)** No termite will be done. **(C)** All cash sales only- no outside financing. 30 day escrow period. Verification of funds required. **(D)** Flood insurance may be required. **(E)** Cracked Slab/Foundation problem. **(F)** City Permit may be required. **(L)** That VA did not remodel this property and does not warrant that any alterations or additions meet local building codes. **(O)** That no public sewer is available. **(T)** Term or Cash only (no outside Financing) verification of funds required. **(TM)** Trading Margin. The properties listed with status TM are available for sale at or above the stated list price. However, reasonable offers (as determined by VA) below the stated prices will be considered for acceptance.
* Contractors Special.

To improve service to program participants, VA will process term offers to purchase property only if the offer includes the following for each purchaser/co-purchaser(s):
1. Offer to purchase– VA form 26-6705. Completed form with original signatures, front and back, plus 2 copies. **2.** Credit Statement – VA Form 6705b (Husband and Wife submit one form) *Submit 1 and 2 only for term offers of 10% or more down* .**3.** Legible copy of the latest year tax return. **4.** Legible copy of latest year W–2 Form. **5.** Most recent pay stub. **6.** If self-employed, year-to-date Profit and Loss Statement signed by an accountant. **7.** Current credit report. Submit evidence that any adverse credit items have been rectified. **8.** If owner occupied, submit deposition of presently owned property, i.e. rental agreement. **9.** For cash offers (personal funds/no outside financing) submit evidence of funds. **Downpayments:** 10% required for non-owner occupied. **Commissions:** paid direct on all sales of less than 10% downpayment. Sales commission checks should not be anticipated until 21 days AFTER the close of escrow. VA pays 6% sales commission on sales which close escrow. Indicate broker's tax ID number on offer. **Offers:** submit cash offers on VA Form 26-6705. A $1,000 Earnest Money Deposit is required on all offers and should be retained in the Brokers Trust account. Submit offers for VA vendee financing on VA Forms 26-6705 and 26-6705b. Submit all offers on triplicate VA Forms (whose provisions along with this as govern). The offer in the best interest of the VA will be processed. VA reserves the right to reject any and all offers and to waive any informality or irregularity in any offers. The name of the successful offereror and sales price will appear in subsequent ads. **Homeless Program:** Properties are available for sale at a discount to eligible homeless providers. Contact us for more details. **All VA properties are sold "as is". No warranties are expressed or implied on the condition of these properties. VA will not be responsible for removal or theft of any items from the properties.**

Sales to VA Affiliates: Purchasers identified in any of the following categories may not have their offers considered on an equal basis with non-affiliates. An affiliate is identified as: VA employees assigned to the Los Angeles VA Regional Office; property management brokers purchasing VA-owned properties which they are managing for VA; fee appraisers purchasing properties on which they have performed a default appraisal for VA; owners, partners, officers, employees, business associates, agents, and any persons performing services for a fee on subject property; close family members of all of the previous categories. Purchase offers received from VA affiliates will not be eligible for consideration until the end of the competitive period and then only if there were no acceptable non-affiliate offers received.

chance of success! The decision-making process usually takes about two weeks, and then you, the winning buyer, are notified by mail.

VA Repos at Auction

Sometimes you'll see VA repos advertised for sale at auction in your local newspaper. There will be an inspection period several days before the auction when you can go and check out the property. You'll be able to pick up guidelines for submitting a bid on the spot. Then the procedure follows the same steps as outlined above.

A Few Reminders about VA Repos

• If there are lots of VA repos available, it's probably a buyer's market. Shop around and compare to get the best deal!

• Compare the price of any home you're thinking about buying with the price of other homes in the area. Make sure the home you're getting is priced WELL BELOW other homes on the market!

• Many VA repos have sat vacant for months or longer. Be cautious about purchasing a VA repo that has sat vacant for more than one winter.

• The VA does not guarantee these homes in any way, shape, or form. Once the home is yours, it's yours for better or for worse. So a thorough property inspection by a qualified home inspector is a must!

Insider's Tip:

When you're buying a VA repo from a veteran, make sure that the veteran has owned the property for at least one month. Why? Because it takes a month or more for the lender to receive the official VA guarantee on the loan. If the sale is made too quickly, you might miss the boat—and the existing VA loan may not be considered part of the sale!

Chapter 12:
FDIC Sales

You've probably heard of the FDIC—or Federal Deposit Insurance Corporation—down at your local bank. The FDIC is the organiza tion that protects your money in banks that are federally insured. If your bank fails, the FDIC takes over the bank's assets and your deposits are insured up to $100,000.

When banks fail, they unleash more foreclosed properties onto the market. Many of these properties are taken over by the FDIC and then re-sold. These days, with more and more banks failing, there are literally thousands of listings to choose from—everything from single-family homes to mobile homes and multi-family homes.

Sales of these homes are handled by the FDIC's Division of Liquidation, or DOL. The FDIC is known for bargains galore, especially on fixer-uppers. Sometimes you can obtain these properties for as little as 50 cents on the dollar! This chapter will tell you how to find these deals and take advantage of them!

Affordable Housing Program

The FDIC even has an Affordable Housing Program, which reserves certain properties for purchase by families with low to moderate incomes. To qualify, the appraised value of a single-family home must usually be less than $105,000.

As the potential buyer, you must agree to live in the home for at least a year. Your gross household income for the next year must also not exceed 115% of the median income for your area. In practical terms, this means that your income must be no more than moderate for your area—there must be an equal number of people who make less than you do, and who make more than you do. This income requirement is adjusted for family size, so if you have a large family you may be eligible even if your income appears to be higher than the median. Contact your regional FDIC office for more information. (See the list of FDIC offices in this chapter.)

Insider's Tip:

If you are an existing tenant in an FDIC property, you are eligible to purchase the property WHETHER OR NOT your income qualifies! Now THAT'S truly the opportunity of a lifetime!

Getting the Scoop on FDIC Houses

Call one of the offices listed at the end of this chapter and ask to speak to the "real estate owned" (REO) or liquidation division. Leave your name and address, as well as the type of property you are interested in, and they will send you a property list in 10 working days. This list includes each property's address, asking price, and the name of the person who will handle the sale. See the sample list on the next page.

After you examine the list and decide which property you want, call the FDIC office again and tell them which property you're interested in. They'll look it up on their computer and direct you to the right broker or FDIC accountant, who will help you take things from there.

FDIC sales are advertised in the local newspapers and broadcast media when a sale is going to be held. Sales are also listed in *The Wall Street Journal*. So keep your eyes open and be ready to jump on these super deals!

FDIC Properties at Auction

Occasionally, FDIC properties go on the auction block. Lists of these properties may be obtained from your local FDIC office, along with auction dates, times, and information on how to register.

FDIC Sample Property List

REAL ESTATE OWNED PROPERTY LISTINGS
SINGLE FAMILY RESIDENTIAL

LAMIS NO. PROPERTY ADDRESS	DESCRIPTION	MARKETING PRICE	CONTACT
ALTADENA, CALIFORNIA			
4601/501222351 SFR	SFR PLUS LOT	$315,000.00	REALTY WORLD
LAGUNA NIGUEL, CALIFORNIA			
4454/004202501 SFR	4BD/3BA 2,831 SQ.FT. 3 CAR GARAGE IN ESCROW		RE/MAX SOUTH COUNTY
LOS ANGELES, CALIFORNIA			
4601/501222251 SFR	THREE LEVEL 4,005 SQ. FT. IN ESCROW		RE/MAX
MALIBU, CALIFORNIA			
4598/004258391 SFR	6,565 SQ. FT. SFR APPROX. 95% COMPLETE IN ESCROW		JON DOUGLAS REAL ESTA
MORENO VALLEY, CALIFORNIA			
4454/500661761 SFR	3/1 HAS GUEST HOUSE, TOTAL 4.75 ACRES		KENNEDY-WILSON
OCEANSIDE, CALIFORNIA			
4602/501224891 SFR	4BR/2.5BA APPROX. 2,895 SQ. FT. IN ESCROW		COLDWELL BANKER
4615/501265321 SFR	SFR IN ESCROW		RANCH & SEA

The sealed-bid procedure is commonly used at these auctions, which means you must submit a bid before the auction day by mail. When the envelopes are opened, the highest bidder wins.

Don't neglect the home inspection and research portion of your mission BEFORE you place your bid! Read the fine print and ask plenty of questions—the success of your bid depends on it!

Making an Offer

FDIC properties are sold "as is," which means you should follow the same process of researching your potential home before you make an offer as outlined in Chapter 6. The FDIC suggests that you have a professional inspection of the property done before you commit yourself to a bid.

FDIC properties are most often sold at their appraised value, but the accountant or broker assigned to your property will work with you to get the price down. Try starting out with an offer 10% to 15% below the listed price. If your research and inspection of the home warrants it, you could go as low as 30% below list. Then, get ready to sit back and wait—it may take as long as 30 to 60 days before you know if your offer has been accepted.

We know a woman who received the FDIC property list and lo and behold, found a home she wanted to bid on. She did her property inspection and found that the home needed some plumbing work done, as well as some cosmetic repairs. She put in an offer at 20% of the listed price, and ended up getting the property at 15% below list. It was a sweet deal for her, and she used the money she saved to fix up the property!

As the buyer, you must arrange your own financing. This task will be easy if you refer back to Chapters 3 and 4 in this book. The FDIC accountant or broker you're working with is sure to have some helpful suggestions.

This chapter concludes with a list of FDIC offices by region. There are plenty of great FDIC properties out there just waitin' for the takin'—so go get 'em!

FDIC Regional Offices – Division of Supervision

Atlanta Regional Office
(Alabama, Florida, Georgia,
North Carolina, South
Carolina, Virginia, West
Virginia)
One Atlantic Center, Suite
1600
1201 W. Peachtree St., N.E.
Atlanta, GA 30309
(404) 817-1300

Boston Regional Office
(Connecticut, Maine,
Massachusetts, New
Hampshire, Rhode Island,
Vermont)
Westwood Executive Center
200 Lowder Brook Dr.
Westwood, MA 02090
(508) 520-7250
(800) 723-0679 ext. 2294

Chicago Regional Office
(Illinois, Indiana, Michigan,
Ohio, Wisconsin)
500 West Monroe St., Suite
3600
Chicago, IL 60661
(800) 944-5343

Dallas Regional Office
(Colorado, New Mexico,
Oklahoma, Texas)
1910 Pacific Ave., Suite 1900
Dallas, TX 75201
(800) 759-9314
(800) 925-3342

Kansas City Regional
Office
(Iowa, Kansas, Minnesota,
Missouri, Nebraska, North
Dakota, South Dakota)
2345 Grand Ave., Suite
1500
Kansas City, MO 64108
(312) 382-6000

Memphis Regional Office
(Arkansas, Kentucky,
Louisiana, Mississippi,
Tennessee)
5100 Poplar Ave., Suite
1900
Memphis, TN 38137
(202) 393-8400

New York Regional Office
(Delaware, District of
Columbia, Maryland, New
Jersey, New York,
Pennysylvania, Puerto Rico,
Virgin Islands)
452 Fifth Ave., 19th Floor
New York, NY 10018
(800) 365-0381

San Francisco Regional
Office
(Alaska, Arizona,
California, Guam, Hawaii,
Idaho, Montana, Nevada,
Oregon, Utah, Washington,
Wyoming)
25 Ecker St., Suite 2300
San Francisco, CA 94105
(800) 234-0867

FDIC Regional Offices –
Divison of Depositor and Asset Services

Northeast Service Center
(Connecticut, Maine, Massachusetts, New Hampshire, New
Jersey, New York, Pennsylvania, Rhode Island, Vermont, Puerto
Rico, Virgin Islands)
111 Founder's Plaza
East Hartford, CT 06108
(203) 290-2000

Southeast Service Center
(Alabama, Delaware, District of Columbia, Florida, Georgia,
Kentucky, Maryland, Mississippi, North Carolina, South
Carolina, Tennessee, Virginia, West Virginia)
One Atlantic Center, Suite 1300
1201 W. Peachtree St., N.E.
Atlanta, GA 30309
(404) 817-2500

Midwest Service Center
(Illinois, Indiana, Iowa, Kansas, Michigan, Minnesota, Missouri,
Nebraska, North Dakota, Ohio, South Dakota, Wisconsin)
500 West Monroe St., Suite 3200
Chicago, IL 60661
(800) 944-5343

Southwest Service Center
(Arkansas, Colorado, Louisiana, New Mexico, Oklahoma,
Texas)
5080 Spectrum Dr., Suite 1000E
Dallas, TX 75248
(214) 991-0039

Western Service Center
(Alaska, Arizona, California, Guam, Hawaii, Idaho, Montana,
Nevada, Oregon, Utah, Washington, Wyoming)
Four Park Plaza
Jamboree Center
Irvine, CA 92714
(714) 263-7765

Chapter 13:
State Surplus Sales

S tate surplus sales are a very specialized area of bargain real estate. They are not as common as some of the other methods of finding discount properties described in this book. But rest assured, incredible deals DO happen in state surplus every day—and the prices are so low, you won't want to miss these deals!

What ARE State Surplus Sales?

When a State agency decides it no longer needs a certain piece of property, the property is returned to the State government to be put on the market. This is often a complicated process for the state—it can take up to a year and a half to complete, because an actual law must be passed that authorizes the State government to dispose of a particular property in this way.

Once the law is passed and goes into effect (which usually happens in the fall months, September or October) the property must first be offered back to the State, then to local counties. If no offers are made, that's when the property can be sold to public bidders like you.

Your state surplus agency also sells other types of real property—things like cars, trucks, boats, planes, and much more. One thing's for sure—you'll find bargains here that you never knew existed, and you might even change your lifestyle in the process!

What Kinds of Properties are Out There?

Most state surplus properties are designed for special use or are large, commercial properties that would make great low-cost housing projects or schools. Open land is often available.

The State does not normally sell single family homes simply because they don't own that many—for example, in California only three homes have been sold this way in the last five years. However, the types of properties available vary quite a bit from state to state. Don't take anything for granted—your state may have deals on bargain homes that are just waiting for buyers like you!

State Historic Properties

Here's a very special category of properties that you can often find available through State Surplus. Usually they are older structures which are classified as State Landmarks. When state governments can't afford the upkeep on these properties, they are sold at auction.

People are buying up these properties and turning them into homes, hotels, bed and breakfasts, and offices. And the best thing about them is their unbelievably low prices! Place a call to your State Surplus Agency to find out more. (See Appendix E at the end of this book.) Depending on what state you're in, they may refer you to the General Services Department, the Historic Preservation Office, or the Parks Department for even more details.

We know from experience that it helps to be very specific about the type of property you're looking for. That way, it's easier for the State to help you find the property you really want! A case in point: a couple we know wanted to buy an older, historic building to turn into a bed and breakfast. They called the State Surplus office in California and asked specifically for a property located in the "Gold Rush" hills behind Sacramento.

That way, the people in the State office were able to keep their eyes and ears open. The last we heard, the couple were happily fixing up their new purchase as a charming historic bed and breakfast—plus, they can live on the premises too!

Tracking Them Down

No doubt about it, you can find GREAT bargains through doing business with the State. The process of locating and buying property from state surplus agencies is very easy to follow, and works like this:

1. The State will advertise any properties they have for sale in your local newspaper. Occasionally they will advertise a very desirable property in *The Wall Street Journal*, so you might also look there.

2. If you see a property you are interested in, call the contact person listed in the ad right away. Ask them to send you a sales brochure about the property.

3. The sales brochure will include all the information the State has about the property, often with photos and descriptions, plus the most recent appraised value. The brochure will also include an "offer form" with specific instructions telling you how to make a bid on the property.

4. Just like with any other discount property, your own research is the key to success! Refer to Chapter 6 in this book to help your personal investigation of the property go smoothly—and please remember to be VERY thorough. The contact person at the State Surplus Agency will also be helpful to you during this phase.

5. Once you are sure you want to acquire the property, you will need to obtain your own financing, complete the offer form, and submit it with a cashier's check for the required down payment. The State Surplus Agency will evaluate all bids received. The highest bidder will be given an option for 60 days to finish up his/her research and obtain financing.

6. If all goes well, and you still want the property, you will now enter into a regular escrow. Within 90 days, the property will be yours!

State Surplus Agencies

Use the list in Appendix E to find the State Surplus Agency nearest you. Ask to speak to the Office of Real Estate and Design. You'll be amazed by the many types of real estate that are offered—and by the incredibly low prices!

Chapter 14:
Rural Properties &
Farmland

Maybe your heart's desire takes you to where the air is clean, the grass smells sweet, and the old mill stream flows down to the local fishing hole. If you want to be at home on the range, or down on the farm, or even just sitting on the porch swing at your very own rural homestead, your dream is closer to reality than you might think!

Both the Federal government and commercial banks are set up to provide assistance to people just like you. And we're not talking about nickels and dimes—we're talking about sizable loans. These agricultural loans are just the ticket for people who like rural living.

The only bad news is that you may have to jump through some hoops to get these loans. The rules, regulations, and requirements surrounding them can be downright ornery! The purpose of this chapter is to help simplify the two major government programs designed to assist people with agricultural loans. So pull up your rocking chair and settle in for a spell while we take a quick spin through agricultural loans!

Goodbye to Farmer's Home Administration

The Farmer's Home Administration (FmHA) had a long history of offering loans for farm operations and rural home ownership. A branch of the U.S. Department of Agriculture, it was established during the Depression to help keep people on the farm. Federal legislation finally put an official end to this agency in October 1994.

Hello to RECD and CFSA

As of December 1994, two brand new agencies, still under the auspices of the U.S. Department of Agriculture, are handling the duties of the now defunct Farmer's Home Administration. Rural Economic and Community Development handles rural home loans, and the Consolidated Farm Service Agency handles farm operating and purchase loans.

Rural Home Loans Through RECD

The new office of Rural Economic and Community Development has a national headquarters:

> Rural Economic and Community Development (RECD)
> U.S. Dept. of Agriculture
> Washington, DC. 20250
> (202) 720-4323

The RECD also maintains state offices. A list of addresses and phone numbers is provided in Appendix F at the end of this book. Keep in mind that there may be many changes in this information during 1995. If you need assistance, call the national office of the RECD at the number listed above.

The Lender of Last Resort

The RECD is known as a "lender of last resort." That means you can only apply to the agency if you are unable to obtain financing from a commercial bank at reasonable rates.

The RECD specializes in loans for rural homes and other types of properties in what is considered "open country." In some cases this means areas with a population up to 25,000, though in most cases we're talking about populations up to 10,000. No doubt about it, we're talking the wide open spaces here!

Who is Eligible for RECD Loans?

Good loan candidates have low to moderate incomes, plus a good credit history and repayment profile. Here are the eligibility requirements:

1. You must be a U.S. citizen or legal alien with permanent residency .

2. You must show a favorable credit history and the ability to pay back the loan; and most importantly,

3. You must fall within the qualifying income range. For a direct loan, you must not exceed what is considered 80% of the median national income (which identifies you as a low-income family). For a guaranteed loan, you must have 115% of the median national income (which identifies you as a moderate-income family). Because these figures vary county by county, ask your state RECD office for the eligibility figures in your county.

Direct vs. Guaranteed Loans

When you apply for an RECD loan, you'll fill out a form that asks questions about where you want to live, your budget, and your ability to repay the loan. The agency will then order and review your credit report.

Your income will determine how big a loan you get. If the RECD says your income is too low for a direct loan, they'll refer you to HUD for a loan from that agency. (See Chapter 5 in this book for information about HUD loans). If your income is too high, they'll refer you to a private lender like the VA for a guaranteed loan. In that case, the RECD may choose to underwrite your loan and guarantee it as a second party.

The RECD will loan you up to 100% of the appraised value of the property for a direct loan—or underwrite up to 90% of the appraised value of the property for a guaranteed loan. Now that's a REAL loan we're talking about, not just some half-baked financing!

Foreclosures for Sale

Foreclosures come up for sale all the time at individual county offices of the RECD. Contact your state RECD office (see Appendix F) to get the phone number of your nearest local office. If a county has five or more properties for sale, they usually choose a private real estate broker to sell the properties like any other kind of traditional real estate.

If no sale takes place within 90 days, other methods of disposing of the property come into play, including public auctions. Often, however, there are long waiting lists of eligible buyers who are registered with the RECD—and they have first priority when it comes to bidding on the properties.

Insider's Tip:

Call the RECD office early in your search and get your name put on the waiting list!

Generally RECD properties offered for public sale are considered "unsuitable" for some reason and need plenty of fixer-upper work. For the most part, they are cash only sales, and they often go to public or non-profit organizations. However, things vary so much from one part of the country to the other that you shouldn't take anything for granted! DO call your RECD office and find out for certain what kinds of properties are up for sale in your area!

Farm Loans through CFSA

As of December 1994, the Consolidated Farm Service Agency is only a name—no national or state offices exist yet. Because this agency is still being formed within the U.S. Dept. of Agriculture, for the time being you must contact the office of Rural Economic and Community Development to inquire about farm loans and properties.

The Consolidated Farm Service Agency was created to make loans for people who want to get started in farming—especially those who can't obtain commercial credit or have limited income. To be eligible for a loan from this agency, you must already be, or want to be, an operator of a "family size" farm or ranch. Loan terms and interest rates are much more favorable than the conventional rates offered through commercial banks. In fact, the U.S. Government, through the Department of Agriculture, is subsidizing these loans to get people back onto the farm.

Who is Eligible?

1. You must be a U.S. citizen or legal alien to be eligible for CFSA loans.
2. You must show the ability to pay back the loan.
3. You must have enough education or farming experience to run a farm.
4. You must be unable to obtain credit at reasonable rates through a commercial bank.
5. You're eligible if you are already the owner operator or tenant operator of a family-size farm at the time of closing.

Loan Terms

Farm Purchase Loans
Maximum 40 years at a current rate of 8.0 % (December 1994)

Operating Loans
1-7 years at a current rate of 7 1/2 % (December 1994)

What You'll Need to Know

The loan officer will want to know if you can run a farm. You'll be asked detailed questions about your operating costs, budgets (labor costs, seed costs, etc.), and crop background. You don't need to have owned a farm before, but you WILL need to "speak the language" about operations, costs, and projections.

Your ability to pay back the loan will be determined by financial statements, tax returns, the ability of your farm to produce cash flow, and whether you have sufficient collateral to guarantee the loan.

Insider's Tip:

This tip came to us from a loan officer, who emphasized how important it is to prepare for your interview ahead of time. For example, you can go to your local county agricultural commission to find out what crops grow well in your area. Talk to other farmers in the area, too!

Forfeited Farm Properties

The Consolidated Farm Service Agency has truckloads of acreage and farms in inventory that have been forfeited due to foreclosure. In 1993, when this agency was still operating as the Farmer's Home Administration, there were over 25,000 foreclosed farms and 8 million acres in inventory!

When it comes to foreclosures, the CFSA has three priorities. The first priority is to get the lost property back to its original owners through new loans. If that doesn't work, priority number two is that the property becomes available for sale to other people eligible for loans through the agency. Finally, priority number three states that foreclosures not eligible for CFSA loan packages—meaning, properties that are not "family-sized farms"—are available for sale to the public by bid.

Until the Consolidated Farm Service Agency offices are firmly in place, you must contact the state offices for Rural Economic and Community Development for information on farm sales in individual counties. See Appendix F for the complete list.

Farm Credit System

If you qualify for commercial credit and are an experienced farmer, you can get a loan from the Farm Credit System to purchase a farm or ranch. <u>Currently, the Farm Credit System provides over $54 billion dollars in loans to over half a million borrowers</u>!

The Farm Credit System dates back to 1916, when it was started to provide credit for American farmers. The money comes from eight commercial banks that provide loans to local credit agricultural cooperative associations. There are over 250 of these associations nationwide. They usually operate on a county level and are owned by the borrowers/stockholders. These associations offer both long and short term loans—including real estate loans, operating loans, and rural home mortgage loans.

How to Apply

To apply for a loan through the Farm Credit System, you must go through the local cooperative associations—not the eight commercial banks, which only broker loans to the associations.

Local agricultural cooperative associations go by various names, such as Production Credit Association or Agricultural Credit Association. If you can't find the phone number of your nearest agricultural credit cooperative, you can order the Farm Credit National Directory from the Farm Credit Council that lists them all. The cost is about $20, including shipping and handling. Call or write:

> Farm Credit Council
> P.O. Box 5130
> Denver, CO 80217-5130
> (303) 740-4200

If you have general questions about the Farm Credit Administration, or want the telephone number of your closest association, you may also call officials at the national office of Farm Credit System:

> Farm Credit Administration
> 1501 Farm Credit Drive
> McClean, VA 22102 - 5090
> (703) 883 - 4000

Who is Eligible for Farm Credit Loans?

Farmers, ranchers, and aquatic producers are the candidates of choice for farm credit loans. Usually you must have a solid background in your field and a good financial history. Other eligible borrowers include owners, or potential owners, of rural homes in areas with a population of less than 2,500. (Note: there's a new law under consideration that would up this population limit to 25,000!).

Remember, although the Farm Credit System is regulated by the U.S. Government, loans from this agency ARE NOT subsidized by the Federal government. <u>These are commercial loans.</u> To qualify you must show a solid credit history, repayment ability, and collateral. If you're applying for a farm loan, add to that management ability, a good operating plan, and the ability to make a profit after you pay your living expenses. The bottom line: these loans are great, but they're not for the faint of heart!

We learned about a man who made the farm loan system work to his advantage. He came from a family of farmers, but always wanted to expand the operation. He started out with a loan from what is now the Consolidated Farm Service Agency, and then "graduated" to a loan from the Farm Credit Administration as he became more successful. Now he's got one of the largest farms in his area, and every harvest time he's packing in the profits! Using these farm loans as a two-tiered system helped him grow his way to success!

Cash in on Farm Credit Bank Foreclosures!

The Farm Credit Bank System has properties for sale that have been forfeited back to the lending associations. These sales are handled by the local associations themselves—not by the regional banks! Each association has their own way of marketing these properties, which are available for purchase by the general public.

Some associations publish quarterly newsletters with property listings. Often sales are negotiated through an association official like an ordinary real estate transaction, with a bid and offers by individuals. Sometimes auctions are held. If you've identified an area where you want to purchase a farm foreclosure, <u>call the Farm Credit Bank office nearest you from the list on the next page</u>. They will give you the phone number of your local association. You can then give them a call and ask to be put on their mailing list, or ask that they notify you in some other way about upcoming sales.

The Time Is Now!

With farm and rural properties available in record numbers, it's never been easier to buy rural acreage. The deals are out there just waiting for you! Get on the phone and call the agencies listed in this chapter on the local, state and national levels—and don't be afraid to ask questions.

You can <u>always</u> find the right person to talk to if you are clear with the agency receptionist about your needs. The people who work for these agencies have a job to do, and that job is to make loans to people like you! They also have properties that they <u>need</u> and <u>want</u> to sell! It all adds up to a situation where you can't lose—unless you don't call!

Farm Credit Banks

Farm Credit Bank of Columbia
P.O. Box 1499
Columbia, SC 29202
(803) 799-5000

AgriBank, FCB
P.O. Box 64949
St. Paul, MN 55164
(612) 282-8800

CoBank, ABC
(Agrabusiness Eastern Division)
(413) 821-0200

Farm Credit Bank of Wichita
P.O Box 2940
Wichita, KS 67201
(316) 266-5100

Farm Credit Bank of Texas
P.O. Box 15919
Austin, TX 78761
(512) 465-0400

Western Farm Credit Bank
P.O. Box 13106-C
Sacramento, CA 95813
(916) 485-6049

AgAmerica, FCB
P.O. Box TAF-C5
Spokane, WA 99220
(509) 838-9300

Chapter 15:
Fannie Mae & Freddie Mac

Fannie Mae and Freddie Mac are legends in their own time. They are the two biggest sources of home loans in the nation! <u>Fannie Mae is responsible for one out of every four home loans, while Freddie Mac is responsible for one out of every eight home loans!</u>

The thing you need to remember is that Fannie Mae and Freddie Mac are secondary mortgage lenders—which means that they are both "invisible" to you, the consumer. They are services used by mortgage lenders—<u>they give other lenders the money, then those lenders give the money to you.</u> Some lenders choose to use Fannie Mae, and others choose to use Freddie Mac. The two are competitors, and that means that sometimes one offers better deals than the other.

So why do you need to know about Fannie Mae and Freddie Mac? The main reason is because they both offer alternative lending programs for low to moderate income home buyers. If that means you, you'll benefit from finding out about these programs yourself BEFORE you sit down with a lender. Remember, knowledge is power!

Plus, a working knowledge of Fannie Mae and Freddie Mac can only help you as you learn about the mortgage process. So here we go!

All About Fannie Mae

Fannie Mae—the nickname for the Federal National Mortgage Association—dates all the way back to 1938. Today it's a huge industry worth between $300-$400 billion a year! Fannie Mae is a private corporation, owned by its stockholders and traded on the stock market.

Fannie Mae uses the money it makes in the stock market to buy up federally insured mortgage loans from a network of over 2,800 lending agencies—which include commercial banks, mortgage banks, and savings and loans. What does this mean to you? Namely, <u>Fannie Mae is the largest source of money for conventional mortgages in the U.S.!</u>

Community Home Buyers Program

This Fannie Mae program is designed to help low to moderate income Americans obtain low-cost home loans. There are many loan options available, but the basic features you get are <u>very flexible terms, minimum cash required at closing, and as little as 5% down!</u>

To qualify for this program, your income must be between 100% to 115% of the median income for your area. The exact amount will vary from area to area. Basically, median income means that there must be an equal number of people in your area who make less than you AND an equal number that make more than you.

For more information on the Community Home Buyers Program, call or write Fannie Mae at:

> Fannie Mae
> 3900 Wisconsin Ave. NW
> Washington, DC 20016
> **(800) 832-2345**

Remember that Fannie Mae is a <u>secondary</u> mortgage lender. You must go through your own local lender to see if you are eligible for a Fannie Mae loan. Your local lender will deal with Fannie Mae directly on your behalf, and tell you the types and terms of Fannie Mae loans that are available.

People at the Fannie Mae offices can't provide loan counseling or other advice—but they CAN tell you everything you need to know about the Community Home Buyers Program in your area!

In addition to contacting the Fannie Mae National Office, you can call the regional office nearest you. See the list on the next page.

Regional Fannie Mae Offices

Northeastern Region
(Connecticut, Delaware, Maine, Massachusetts, New
Hampshire, New Jersey, New York, Pennsylvania, Puerto Rico,
Rhode Islands, Vermont, Virgin Islands)
1900 Market St. Suite 800
Philadelphia, PA 19103
(215) 575-1400

Southeastern Region
(Alabama, Washington D.C., Florida, Georgia, Kentucky,
Maryland, Mississippi, North Carolina, South Carolina,
Tennessee, Virginia, West Virginia)
950 East Paces Ferry Rd.
Atlanta, GA 30326
(404) 398-6000

Midwestern Region
(Illinois, Indiana, Iowa, Michigan, Minnesota, Ohio, Nebraska,
North Dakota, South Dakota, Wisconsin)
One South Wacker Dr.
Chicago, IL 60606
(312) 368-6200

Southwestern Region
(Arkansas, Arizona, Colorado, Kansas, Louisiana, Missouri,
New Mexico, Oklahoma, Texas, Utah)
13455 Noel Rd. Suite 600
#2 Galleria Tower
Dallas, TX 75240
(214) 773-4663

Western Region
(Alaska, California, Guam, Idaho, Montana, Nevada, Oregon,
Washington, Wyoming)
135 North Los Robles Ave. Ste. 300
Pasadena, CA 91101
(818) 396-5100

> ## Insider's Tip:
>
> Fannie Mae officials say it pays to call them first, BEFORE you sit down with your local mortgage lender! Plus, Fannie Mae can send you FREE GUIDES that walk you through the entire home buying process! These guides are called "Opening the Door to a Home of Your Own" and "Choosing the Mortgage That's Right for You." Call (800) 688-HOME to receive your free guides! (See the Fannie Mae ad on the next page.)

Foreclosures Through Fannie Mae

Fannie Mae has its very own REO (real estate owned) program that offers foreclosed properties for sale to the general public. To find out about these properties, call the Fannie Mae regional field office nearest you from the list on the previous page. Ask for the Property Disposal Department and ask them to send you a property list of available REOs.

Usually, Fannie Mae REOs are sold through a network of local real estate brokers. You can find out the names of these brokers from the Fannie Mae representatives in the Property Disposal Department—just ask!

Most of these foreclosure sales are handled just like regular real estate sales. If you're interested in a property, you place an offer with the local real estate broker in charge of the sale. Once in a while, Fannie Mae will use a sealed bid procedure for these sales. If so, the local agent will give you instructions on how to submit your bid.

> ## Insider's Tip:
>
> While the number of REOs offered by Fannie Mae is decreasing, there are plenty of properties being offered by the agency as "fair market" sales. A typical Midwest field office of Fannie Mae offers about 350 properties for sale a year! In other states, like California, you can expect to find even more! AND as we've already seen, the terms on these loans can be GREAT!

At Fannie Mae, we make sure mortgage lenders have money to lend for homes. And we provide information to help you decide if you're ready to buy, and to help you choose a mortgage. For your free guides, call 1-800-688-HOME.

FannieMae
Showing America A New Way Home.

More money available for home buyers

There's good news for families who want to buy their own homes. Fannie Mae, the federal home-mortgage agency, plans to make $1 billion available for home loans over the next six years for low- and moderate-income buyers.

Along with the money, Fannie Mae is putting out new guidelines for lenders who will make the federally backed loans. The whole effort is targeted at would-be home buyers who, until now, could not qualify for a conventional mortgage. Under the new rules, lenders will consider an applicant's "alternative credit" history — records of rent payments, utility accounts and employment histories. Those are

fight back

DAVID HOROWITZ

often the only credit references low-income people have, even though they can afford the monthly loan payments.

Fannie Mae is also reaching out to prospective homeowners with counseling, assistance and information about the new home-loan program. They want to bring in those people who've been turned away by lenders in the past and have given up on owning their own homes. The government plans to reach every renter in America with home-ownership information by the year 2000.

Lenders push for buyer approval

By MARY FRICKER
NYT REGIONAL NEWSPAPERS

Have you been turned down for a home loan lately? Don't give up. That's the message from mortgage lenders as they try to help more Americans realize the dream of home ownership.

"Our goal is that there are no 'nos.' There are only 'laters,'" said Terrance Hodel, president of North American Mortgage Co. in Santa Rosa, the nation's fifth-largest home lender.

"We do whatever we can to help," said Mary Trigg, director of public relations for Home Savings of America, whose headquarters is near Los Angeles. "If our customers don't qualify today, maybe they need to pay down some debt. Our people would work with them."

Part of the push to help potential home buyers qualify for a home loan is coming from Fannie Mae, an agency in Washington that buys 25 percent of the home loans made in the United States each year. Fannie Mae buys the loans from lenders, so lenders then have the money to make more loans.

For two years Hodel has served on Fannie Mae's National Advisory Committee, which meets several times a year in Washington to discuss mortgage issues.

At those meetings, Hodel said, there's a lot of emphasis lately on helping people put their financial houses in order.

"Fannie Mae's stated corporate goal is to get to a 'no nos' future," Hodel said.

FANNIE MAE
SOUTHERN CALIFORNIA PROPERTY LIST
REPORT: PROPRUN.FEX   DATE: 941129

COUNTY	ZIP	PROP TYPE	ADDRESS	CITY	LIST PRICE	BROKER
KERN	93205	SINGL		BODFISH	71,800	COLDWELL BANKER
KERN	93225	SINGL		FRAZIER PARK	73,000	THE LAND OFFICE
KERN	93225	SINGL		FRAZIER PARK	119,000	THE LAND OFFICE
KERN	93225	SINGL		FRAZIER PARK	72,000	THE LAND OFFICE
KERN	93225	SINGL		FRAZIER PARK	114,500	THE LAND OFFICE
KERN	93268	BLANK		TAFT	0	
KERN	93304	SINGL		BAKERSFIELD	77,800	COLDWELL BANKER
KERN	93304	SINGL		BAKERSFIELD	0	
KERN	93306	SINGL		BAKERSFIELD	108,900	COLDWELL BANKER
KERN	93308	SINGL		BAKERSFIELD	132,500	COLDWELL BANKER
KERN	93309	CONDO		BAKERSFIELD	29,500	STOCKDALE MANAGEMENT & REALTY
KERN	93309	SINGL		BAKERSFIELD	74,500	COLDWELL BANKER
KERN	93309	SINGL		BAKERSFIELD	0	
KERN	93312	SINGL		BAKERSFIELD	109,500	COLDWELL BANKER
KERN	93312	SINGL		BAKERSFIELD	131,000	COLDWELL BANKER
KERN	93312	SINGL		BAKERSFIELD	124,900	COLDWELL BANKER
KERN	93313	SINGL		BAKERSFIELD	119,500	STOCKDALE MANAGEMENT & REALTY
KERN	93560	SINGL		ROSAMOND	16,500	TROTH, BW & WB, REALTORS
KERN	93560	SINGL		ROSMOND	101,000	HARVEST PROPERTIES
KERN	93560	SINGL		ROSAMOND	84,500	TROTH, BW & WB, REALTORS
KERN	93561	SINGL		TEHACHAPI	76,600	COLDWELL BANKER - BEST REALTY
KERN	93561	SINGL		TEHACHAPI	118,750	HARVEST PROPERTIES
KERN	93561	SINGL		TEHACHAPI	125,500	HARVEST PROPERTIES
KERN	93561	SINGL		TEHACAPI	102,500	COLDWELL BANKER - BEST REALTY
KERN	93561	SINGL		TEHACHAPI	108,000	COLDWELL BANKER - BEST REALTY
LOS ANGELES	90001	MULTI		LOS ANGELES	110,000	BUNKER HILL REAL ESTATE
LOS ANGELES	90002	SINGL		LOS ANGELES	0	
LOS ANGELES	90002	SINGL		LOS ANGELES	55,000	REALTY WORLD - RAINBOW
LOS ANGELES	90003	SINGL		LOS ANGELES	99,500	BUNKER HILL REAL ESTATE
LOS ANGELES	90003	MULTI		LOS ANGELES	199,500	BUNKER HILL REAL ESTATE
LOS ANGELES	90003	MULTI		LOS ANGELES	179,500	BUNKER HILL REAL ESTATE
LOS ANGELES	90003	CONDO		LOS ANGELES	189,500	BUNKER HILL REAL ESTATE
LOS ANGELES	90004	MULTI		LOS ANGELES	145,000	REALTY WORLD/JOHNSON & JOHNSON
LOS ANGELES	90004	MULTI		LOS ANGELES	174,900	COLDWELL BANKER
LOS ANGELES	90004	SINGL		LOS ANGELES	0	
LOS ANGELES	90005	SINGL		LOS ANGELES	45,000	PRUDENTIAL L.A.
LOS ANGELES	90006	MULTI		LOS ANGELES	139,900	R. S. COOPER

Freddie Mac

Now we come to the second member of the Dynamic Loan Duo—Freddie Mac. Freddie Mac is short for the Federal National Mortgage Association. Founded in 1970, it's the kid brother of Fannie Mae. Just like Fannie Mae, Freddie Mac is a private corporation that provides money to lenders, who in turn pass the money on as loans to you, the home buyer.

To receive brochures about Freddie Mac loan programs and general information about these programs, call Freddie Mac Corporation Communications at (703) 903-2446. There are other numbers you can call for information, too, like the Freddie Mac Customer Service Line at **(800) 424-5401.** Freddie Mac regional offices are listed below. The National Headquarters is:

Freddie Mac
8200 Jones Brent Dr.
McClean, VA 22102
(703) 903-2000

Freddie Mac Regional Offices

Northeastern Region
1410 Springhill Rd.
McClean, VA 22102
(703) 902-7700

Southeastern Region
2339 Paces Ferry Rd.
Atlanta, GA 30839
(404) 438-3800

North Central Region
333 West Wacker Dr.
Chicago, IL 60606
(312) 407-7400

Southwestern Region
12222 Merit Dr., Four Forest Plaza
Dallas, TX 75251
(214) 702-2000

Western Region
21700 Oxnard St.
Woodland Hills, CA 91367
(310) 710-3000

Freddie Mac's Affordable Gold Loans

Affordable Gold loans are designed especially for low and moderate income families—with the added attraction that you DON'T have to be a first-time home buyer to qualify! Typical terms include a mere 5% down with extra options on how you can come up with the down payment—for example, you can take 3% from your own funds and 2% from grants or gifts. Contact your local mortgage lender, or call or write Freddie Mac for more details!

New Loans from Freddie Mac

In April 1994, Freddie Mac created what they call the NeighborWorks loan, which is especially for families with low to moderate incomes. This loan features a LOW, LOW down payment of 5%! To find out more about this loan program, you must go through your neighborhood housing service. Look under Housing Authority or Department of Housing under City Government in your phone book.

In the Summer of 1994, Freddie Mac started YET ANOTHER new loan program called HomeWorks. This program is currently available only in Los Angeles, but it is going to be extended throughout the country soon! The HomeWorks loan is for first-time homeowners, and it offers yet another LOW, LOW, LOW down payment. For information on HomeWorks, and to find out if the program has reached your area yet, contact your local mortgage lender.

Charting Your Course

Like the Fannie Mae program, you'll have to go directly to your local lender to see if you're eligible for Freddie Mac loans. But don't hesitate to write or call Freddie Mac and gather information on their loan programs first! Just like with Fannie Mae, the more background you have, the better your chances of getting an UNBEATABLE DEAL on a home loan!

Freddie Mac REOs

Foreclosed properties, or REOs, are no stranger to Freddie Mac. There's a fine selection of properties to be had. The catch with Freddie Mac is, they won't mail you a list! BUT, you can call the Freddie Mac Customer Service line at **(800) 373-3343**, extension 6, and ask the agent on the phone to tell you about REOs available by state or city. They're give you the location of the property and the Realtor to contact right then and there!

Chapter 16:
SBA Sales

The Small Business Administration (SBA) is known for offering advice and loans to owners of small businesses—but little do most people know that they ALSO have a National Office of Liquidation that oversees the sales of foreclosed properties!

And that doesn't just mean retail shops and restaurants—the SBA has homes for sale, too! In fact, one SBA official told us, "Our properties are all over the map—from residential, commercial and farmland to retail, wholesale and storage." You can see that there's the potential for some REAL bargains in real estate here—and some you can even live in!

SBA Secrets

One reason this branch of the SBA is such a well-kept secret is because the SBA has a vested interest in NOT selling forfeited real estate—if they do, it means their advice and loans have failed! Perhaps this also explains why the SBA is not the most user-friendly agency when it comes to real estate sales. However, when there's a will there's a way—and the fact is, there are SBA agents in place just waiting to sell foreclosed properties to buyers like you!

The SBA's goal in selling real estate is the MAXIMUM recovery of funds with the MINIMUM loss to taxpayers. This means that the SBA will not dump properties onto the market at incredibly discounted rates. The SBA generally offers real estate at fair market value or up to 5% under fair market value. They are also willing to sit on a property to wait for a favorable sale, even up to a year.

But this is the official party line. YOU, who by now know more than most people about buying bargain homes, can probably guess the truth—

there are LOTS of SBA properties out there that sell for less!

The "Little Guy" Advantage

The good news is that the SBA <u>wants</u> to accommodate serious potential "occupier/users," and the agency sells most of its properties in individual lots—that is, not grouped with multiple properties that are too expensive for most ordinary buyers.

<u>This means that the SBA would rather deal with the little guy, namely YOU, than an investor.</u> In fact, if the SBA thinks you're an investor, you DEFINITELY won't get a hero's welcome!

Who to Call

For more information about SBA sales, call or write the national offices of the SBA at:

> Small Business Administration
> 409 Third St., SW.
> Washington, DC 20416
> (202) 205-7501 or (202) 205-7713

The SBA Office of Liquidation can be reached at the same address, with a direct phone line of (202) 205-6500. <u>The SBA also has an 800 information line at (800) 827-5722, which is a good place to start.</u>

Or, call the Regional Field Office nearest you. See the list below. Ask for more information about property sales. They'll probably direct you to an SBA district or field office that's in your own backyard—with great properties available right in your area!

SBA Ins and Outs

Field and district SBA offices handle sales of forfeited properties, with procedures varying from state to state. Some west coast offices, and offices in

SBA Regional Field Offices

Region 1
155 Federal St., Ninth Floor
Boston, MA 02110
(617) 451-2023

Region II
26 Federal Plaza, Room 31-08
New York, NY 10278
(212) 264-1450

Region III
475 Allendale Rd., Suite 201
King Of Prussia, PA 19406
(610) 962-3700

Region IV
1375 Peachtree St. N.E., Fifth Floor
Atlanta, GA 30367
(404) 347-2797

Region V
300 S. Riverside Plaza, Suite 1975 S
Chicago, IL 60606
(312) 353-5000

Region VI
8625 King George Dr., Bldg. C
Dallas, TX 75235
(214) 767-7633

Region VII
911 Walnut St., 13th Floor
Kansas City, MO 64106
(816) 426-3608

Region VIII
633 17th St., 7th Floor
Denver, CO 80202
(303) 294-7186

Region IX
71 Stevenson St., 20th Floor
San Francisco, CA 94105
(415) 744-6402

Region X
2601 Fourth Ave., Room 440
Seattle, WA 98121
(206) 553-5676

Other Offices:
85 Marconi Blvd. #512
Columbus, OH 43215
(614) 469-7325

1240 E. 9th St.
Cleveland, OH 44199
(216) 522-4167

many other states, offer inventory sales lists that you can get by asking for the Control Clerk at the Portfolio Management Division.

Generally, real estate properties are listed with local brokers. Some states require that the SBA advertise properties in the legal section of your local newspaper—look under headings like "Legal Foreclosure." SBA auctions are mainly used for commercial properties. For auctions, the SBA mainly uses licensed local auctioneers, which means you can look in the yellow pages under Auctioneers and call for more info. When you call, ask to be put on the mailing list for foreclosed property sales.

We know one widow who stumbled on an SBA foreclosure listing in her local newspaper. With her kids grown and gone, she was looking to move from her big rambling house to a smaller, more sedate place where she could indulge her interest in antiques. The property for sale was a quaint Victorian house at the north end of Main Street that used to have an antique shop! She bought the place for a song and now opens one room of the house to tourists on weekends—selling a few antiques and making some friends in the process!

Insider's Tip:

SBA district and field offices are required to report all foreclosed real estate available for sale to the public on a nationwide computerized listing. Call the national office of the SBA for information—that's (800) 827-5722.

How Many Properties are Out There?

The number of SBA foreclosed properties varies from district to district. For example, the Los Angeles area may have 60 properties available at any one time, for a total of 200 properties a year—while another, smaller district may offer just one or two properties every few months.

Never Say Never

Even though the stated purpose of the SBA is to sell forfeited properties at fair market value or only 5% under fair market value, it's DEFINITELY safe to assume that SBA properties will sell for less than this—especially those that go to auction. Call your district or field SBA office to find out specific selling practices for your state.

Get your push-button fingers ready—this is one agency with lots of phone menus! In some of the larger regions, it might take you awhile to get a real person on the other end. But persistence and a polite attitude will get you where you want to go as you navigate the SBA!

Chapter 17:
Home Inspection Tips

Now, a word to the wise—no matter what kind of foreclosure or bargain home you buy, be sure to conduct a HOME INSPECTION first! Sometimes, part of the trade-off of getting a bargain price is having to make repairs of one kind or another. You need to know EXACTLY what you're getting for BEFORE you make an offer on the property.

Start out by doing an inspection of the home yourself. This chapter will tell you how. If you become suspicious of potential problems during your own inspection, you may want to hire a professional.

Some government housing and loan programs will require an inspection by a licensed professional. If this is the case, they can direct you to a list of approved inspectors, or you can contact the American Society of Home Inspectors (ASHI) for a list of inspectors in your area. Call or write them at:

American Society of Home Inspectors
655 15th St. NW, Suite 320
Washington, DC 20005
800-743-2744

The Do-It-Yourself Inspection

Here's how to do your own inspection of a property. Using this technique, you can decide whether you REALLY want to place an offer! Arrange a time for your inspection through the Realtor or other person who represents the property. If at all possible, make it a time during the day when the property owners won't be home. You want plenty of daylight, and you want to be free to poke around at your leisure! Bring the following items with you:

- Paper and pencil
- Tape measure
- Flashlight
- Binoculars (great for inspecting the roof!)

Start with the Outside

Begin your inspection by walking completely around the house. Make notes about what you see and write down any questions you have. Here's what to look for:

- Foundation. Are there any cracks in the foundation? If you find cracks bigger than a hairline, they could signal a real problem. Vertical cracks mean structural problems that can be expensive to fix!

- Chimney. Is the chimney straight? Are there cracks, or any loose or missing bricks? Tilted chimneys are dangerous!

- Porches, Patios, and Walkways. If these are concrete, are they free of cracks? If they are next to the foundation, do they fit tightly? Make sure there's no place where water leaks down next to the foundation.

- House Siding and Trim. If these are made of wood, look for signs of rot and termite damage.

- Gutters and Downspouts. The job of gutters and downspouts is to direct water away from the roof and foundation. Are they properly attached and in good working condition?

- Roof. Get out your binoculars for a closer look. What shape are the shingles in? Are they curling or loose—or even missing? If the little rock granules on asphalt shingles have worn off, that means you'll need a new roof soon. Does the roof sag or is it uneven? If so, there might be serious structural problems!

- Windows and Doors. Do they fit tightly? Is there caulking and weather stripping? Are there screens and storm windows, and if so, are they in good condition?

• Garage. Check the walls and roof of the garage the same as you did for the house. Open and close the garage door to make sure it works.

• Crawl space. If there is one, examine it with your flashlight. Look at the foundation and the floor supports above. Check for signs of rot or termite damage. If the furnace and water heater are here, check them out too.

• Yard. How does the lot slope? Does water collect near the foundation? If so, that's a bad sign. Water should drain away from the house. If there is a septic system or a sprinkler system, ask about them, too.

Inside the House

The key to a successful inspection inside the house is to shed plenty of light on the subject! Do your inspection during broad daylight. Turn on the lights and use your flashlight, too. Open all the drapes and move things around as needed so you can do a complete inspection. Use your eyes, ears, and nose to the fullest—if you see, hear, or smell anything suspicious, write it down!

• Floors, Ceilings, and Walls. Are the floors level and solid? (Don't be afraid to jump around a bit!) Check the ceilings and walls for cracks and loose plaster. Stains are a sign of leaks—make a note of them!

• Kitchen. Do the appliances work? Turn them all on to make sure! Is there any sign of water leaks or water damage around the sink or dishwasher? Is there enough counter space and cupboard space?

• Bathrooms. Look closely for signs of water damage here. Check the tile in shower and tub areas for cracks and leaks. Press the tile walls—do they give? If so, that's a bad sign. Check to see if the floor is uneven from water damage, especially around the toilet. Check under the sink for water stains and rot.

• Floor Coverings and Carpet. If there are wood floors, are they in good condition? How about vinyl or linoleum—is it cracked, peeling, or stained? Is the carpet acceptable to you or would you need to replace it?

• Attic. Climb up to the attic and use your flashlight to do a complete inspection. Check the insulation—is it adequate? Are there vents in the attic, and are they properly covered with screens? Stains can be a sign of leaks in the roof. Look for any signs of insect damage, or damage by small animals or birds.

• Basement. Be sure to go down in the basement! If the basement is damp or wet, that's a serious problem! Look for rusty nails or stains that might indicate previous flooding. If the basement is recently painted, some-one might be trying to cover up a former problem—ask for details! If you're not sure if the basement is OK, come back and do another inspection after the next heavy rain!

Check the Home's Major Systems

• Plumbing. Inspect the areas where water and sewer lines come onto the property. Are there trees around whose roots might cause problems with sewer lines? Turn on more than one faucet at the same time to check water pressure. Flush all the toilets. Look for an installation tag on the hot water heater that will tell you its age. Most hot water heaters last about ten years.

Rust or corrosion are danger signals. Is the water heater gas or electric? Is it big enough to meet your needs?

• Heating or Air Conditioning Systems. If the home is in an area where energy costs are high, you want to make sure the home's heating or air conditioning is energy efficient and well maintained. If you're not sure, you can always get someone from the utility company to come out for free and check the system for you. Make sure that all rooms in the home get enough warm or cool air as needed!

• Electrical System. If you're buying an older home that requires the addition of major electrical appliances, you may need to add 220 wiring. The circuit breaker will show you whether the house currently carries 220 volt. If you're not sure about the safety of an electrical system in an older house, get a professional inspection. Check to see if there are enough electrical outlets. The ideal is an outlet every 12 feet or so.

• Environmental Hazards. Some problems like radon, asbestos, and lead paint are hard to detect—but they may be serious enough to keep you from buying a home that otherwise seems OK! Lead paint is common in homes built before 1940; if you have young children, you would need to get the lead paint removed completely before you move in—which can be an expensive and time-consuming procedure. Testing is available for radon and asbestos. If you suspect any of these problems, consult a professional home inspector.

Conclusion

By now you've come a long way in learning about the world of foreclosure properties and discount homes. You have all the tools you need to begin a successful search. If you add a little persistence and determination, you'll be sure to succeed!

But Wait—There's More!

Don't forget to use the material in the Appendices to contact the regional offices of various government agencies near you. The Glossary is always waiting if you need help with a particular term or phrase. And if you have the urge to read even more, the sources in the Bibliography will be of great interest to you!

When you're looking for specific properties available RIGHT NOW in your area, you'll want to refer to your complimentary copy of Volume 2 of *How To Buy Government Foreclosures*. Volume 2 is the perfect companion to this book, because it gives you up-to-date listings of the very foreclosure and bargain properties that you've been reading about here! We think you'll agree—it's a winning combination that will make <u>YOU</u> a winner!

Let Us Hear From You!

We are always seeking to improve the quality of the information included in this volume. If you have suggestions, comments, or success stories to share with us, let us hear from you! Simply send to: Success Stories, Clarendon House , Inc., 1919 State Street, Suite 112, Santa Barbara, CA 93101, Attention Rebecca Harris. To show you our appreciation, we'll send you a FREE publication that will be of GREAT INTEREST to you!

Appendix A: HUD Regional & Field Offices

REGION 1 (BOSTON)

BOSTON REGIONAL OFFICE
Thomas P. O'Neill, Jr. Federal Building
10 Causeway Street, Room 375
Boston, Massachusetts 02222-1092
617.565.5234
800.475.5628 Hotline

FIELD OFFICES
Bangor Office
Casco Northern Bank Building
First Floor
99 Franklin Street
Bangor, Maine 04401-4318
207.945.0467

Burlington Office
Federal Building
11 Elmwood Avenue, Room 244
Post Office Box 879
Burlington, Vermont 05402-0879
802.951.6290

Hartford Office
330 Main Street, First Floor
Hartford, Connecticut 06106-1860
203.240.4522

Manchester Office
Norris Cotton Federal Building
275 Chestnut Street
Manchester, New Hampshire 03101-2487
603.666.7681

Providence Office
Amica Building
10 Weybosset Street
Providence, Rhode Island 02903-1785
401.528.5351

REGION II (NEW YORK)

New York Regional Office
26 Federal Plaza
New York, New York 10278-0068
212.264.6500

FIELD OFFICES:
Albany Office
52 Corporate Circle
Albany, New York 12203-5121
518.464.4200

Buffalo Office
Lafayette Court, Fifth Floor
465 Main Street
Buffalo, New York 14203-1780
716.846.5755

Camden Office
Hudson Building
800 Hudson Square, 2nd Floor
Camden, New Jersey 08102-1156
609.757.5081

Newark Office
One Newark Center
13th Floor
Newark, New Jersey 07102-5260
201.877.1622

REGION III (PHILADELPHIA)

Pennsylvania State Office
Wanamaker Bldg.
100 Penn Square East
Philadelphia, Pennsylvania 19107-3380
215.656.0500

FIELD OFFICES:
Baltimore Office
10 South Howard Street
Baltimore, Maryland 21201-2505
410.962.2520

Charleston Office
405 Capitol Street, Suite 708
Charleston, West Virginia 25301-1795
304.347.7000

Pittsburgh Office
Old Post Office Courthouse
7th Avenue and Grant Street
Pittsburgh, Pennsylvania 15219-1906
412.644.6428

Richmond Office
The 3600 Center
3600 West Broad Street
Post Office Box 90331
Richmond, Virginia 23230-0331
804.278.4507

Washington D.C. Office
820 First Street N.E.
Union Center Plaza
Washington, D.C. 20002-4205
202.275.9200

Wilmington Office
824 Market Street, Suite 850
Wilmington, Delaware 19801-3016
302.573.6300

REGION IV (ATLANTA)

Georgia State Office
Richard B. Russell Federal Building
75 Spring Street, S.W.
Atlanta, Georgia 30303-3388
404.331.4113

FIELD OFFICES:

Birmingham Office
Beacon Ridge Tower
600 Beacon Parkway West, Suite 300
Birmingham, Alabama 35209-3144
205.290.7617

Caribbean Office
New San Juan Office Building
159 Carlos Chardon Avenue
Hato Rey, Puerto Rico 00918-1804
809.766.6121

Columbia Office
Strom Thurmond Federal Building
1835-45 Assembly Street
Columbia, South Carolina 29201-2480
803.253.3202

Coral Gables Office
Gables 1 Tower 1320 South Dixie Highway
Coral Gables, Florida 33146-2911
305.662.4500

Greensboro Office
2306 West Meadowview Road
Greensboro, North Carolina 27407-3707
910.547.4080 or
910.547.4081

Jackson Office
Doctor A.H. McCoy Federal Building
100 West Capital Street, Suite 910
Jackson, Mississippi 39269-1096
601.965.5308

Jacksonville Office
301 West Bay Street, #2200
Jacksonville, Florida 32202-5121
904.232.2626

Knoxville Office
John J. Duncan Federal Building
Third Floor
710 Locust Street, S.W.
Knoxville, Tennessee 37902-2526
615.545.4384

Louisville Office
601 West Broadway
Post Office Box 1044
Louisville, Kentucky 40201-1044
502.582.5251

Memphis Office
One Memphis Place
200 Jefferson Avenue, Suite 1200
Memphis, Tennessee 38103-2335
901.544.3367

Nashville Office
251 Cumberland Bend Drive, Suite 200
Nashville, Tennessee 37228-1803
615.736.5213

Orlando Office
Langley Building
3751 Maguire Boulevard, Suite 270
Orlando, Florida 32803-3032
407.648.6441

Tampa Office
Timberlake Federal Building Annex
501 East Polk Street, Suite 700
Tampa, Florida 33602-3945
813.228.2501

REGION V (CHICAGO)

Chicago Regional Office
Ralph Metcalfe Federal Building
77 West Jackson Boulevard
Chicago, Illinois 60604-3507
312.353.5680

FIELD OFFICES:

Cincinnati Office
Federal Office Building
550 Main Street, Room 9002
Cincinnati, Ohio 45202-3253
513.684.2884

Cleveland Office
One Playhouse Square
1350 Euclid Avenue, Room 420
Cleveland, Ohio 44114-1670
216.522.4065

Columbus Office
200 North High Street
Columbus, Ohio 43215-2499
614.469.6906

Detriot Office
Patrick V. McNamara Federal Building
477 Michigan Avenue
Detroit, Michigan 48226-2592
313.226.7900

Flint Office
605 North Saginaw Street, Room 200
Flint, Michigan 48502-1953
313.766.5112
Grand Rapids Office
2922 Fuller Avenue, N.E.
Grand Rapids, Michigan 49505-3409
616.456.2100

Indianapolis Office
151 North Delaware Street
Indianapolis, Indiana 46204-2526
317.226.6303

Milwaukee Office
Henry S. Reuss Federal Plaza
310 West Wisconsin Avenue, Suite 1380
Milwaukee, Wisconsin 53203-2289
414.297.3214

Minneapolis-St. Paul Office
220 Second Street, South
Minneapolis, Minnesota 55401-2195
612.370.3000

Springfield Office
509 West Capitol Street, Suite 206
Springfield, Illinois 62704-1906
217.492.4085

REGION VI (FORT WORTH)

Fort Worth Regional Office
1600 Throckmorton
Post Office Box 2905
Fort Worth, Texas 76113-2905
817.885.5401
800.827.1240 Hotline

FIELD OFFICES:

Albuquerque Office
625 Truman Street, N.E.
Albuquerque, New Mexico 87110-6443
505.262.6463

Dallas Office
525 Griffin Street, Room 860
Dallas, Texas 75202-5007
214.767.8359

Houston Office
Norfolk Tower
2211 Norfolk, Suite 200
Houston, Texas 77098-4096
713.834.3274

Little Rock Office
TCBY Tower, Suite 900
425 West Capitol Avenue
Little Rock, Arkansas 72201-3488
501.324.5931

Lubbock Office
Federal Office Building
1205 Texas Avenue
Lubbock, Texas 79401-4093
806.743.7265

New Orleans Office
Hale Boggs Federal Bldg.
501 Magazine St. 9th Floor
New Orleans, Louisiana 70130-3099
504.589.7200

San Antonio Office
Washington Square
800 Dolorosa Street
San Antonio, Texas 78207-4563
210.229.6800

Shreveport Office
401 Edward St. Suite 1510
Shreveport, Louisiana 71101-3107
318.676.3385

Tulsa Office
Boston Place
50 E. 15th Street
Tulsa, Oklahoma 74119-4030
918.581.7434

REGION VII (KANSAS CITY)

Great Plains Office
Gateway Tower II
400 State Avenue, Room 200
Kansas City, Kansas 66101-2406
913.551.6864

FIELD OFFICES:
Des Moines Office
Federal Building
210 Walnut Street, Room 239
Des Moines, Iowa 50309-2155
515.284.4512

Omaha Office
Executive Tower Centre
10909 Mill Valley Road
Omaha, Nebraska 68154-3955
402.492.3100

St. Louis Office
Robert A. Young Federal Building
Third Floor
1222 Spruce Street, Room 3207
St. Louis, Missouri 63103-2836
314.539.6583

REGION VIII (DENVER)

Denver Office
First Interstate Tower N.
633 17th Street
Denver, Colorado 80202-3609
303.672.5258
303.672.5057 Hotline

FIELD OFFICES:
Casper Office
4225 Federal Office Building
100 East B Street
Casper, Wyoming 82602-1918
307.261.5252

Fargo Office
Federal Building
653 Second Avenue, North
Post Office Box 2483
Fargo, North Dakota 58108-2483
701.239.5136

Helena Office
Federal Office Building
Drawer 10095
301 South Park, Room 340
Helena, Montana 59626-0095
406.449.5205

Salt Lake City Office
257 E. 200 South, Suite 550
257 Tower Building
Salt Lake City, Utah 84111-2048
801.524.5379

Sioux Falls Office
2400 West 49th Street, #I-201
Sioux Falls, South Dakota 57105-6558
605.330.4223

REGION IX (SAN FRANCISCO)

California State Office
Philip Burton Federal Building and U.S. Courthouse
450 Golden Gate Avenue
Post Office Box 36003
San Francisco, California 94102-3448
415.436.6442
800.935.2279

Indian Programs Office, Region IX
2 Arizona Center
400 North Fifth Street, Suite 1650
Phoenix, Arizona 85004-2361
602.379.4156

FIELD OFFICES:
Fresno Office
1630 East Shaw Avenue, Suite 138
Fresno, California 93710-8193
209.487.5033
800.683.1265 Hotline

Honolulu Office
Seven Waterfront Plaza
500 Ala Moana Boulevard, Suite 500
Honolulu, Hawaii 96813-4918
808.522.8175

Las Vegas Office
1500 East Tropicana Avenue, Suite 205
Las Vegas, Nevada 89119-6516
702.388.6500

Los Angeles Office
1615 West Olympic Boulevard
Los Angeles, California 90015-3801
213.251.7122

Phoenix Office
2 Arizona Center
400 North Fifth Street, Suite 1600
Post Office Box 13468
Phoenix, Arizona 85004-2361
602.379.4434

Reno Office
1575 Delucchi Lane, Suite 114
Post Office Box 30050
Reno, Nevada 89502-6581
702.784.5356

Sacramento Office
777 12th Street, Suite 200
Sacramento, California 95814-1997
916.498.5230

San Diego Office
Mission City Corporate Center
2365 Northside Drive
Suite 300
San Diego, California 92108-2712
619.557.5310

Santa Ana Office
Suite 500
3 Hutton Centre
Santa Ana, California 92707-5764
714.957.3741

Tucson Office
Security Pacific Bank Plaza
33 North Stone Avenue, Suite 700
Tucson, Arizona 85701-1467
602.670.5220

REGION X (SEATTLE)

Seattle Office
Suite 200
Seattle Federal Office Building
909 1st Avenue
Seattle, Washington 98104-1000
206.220.5101

FIELD OFFICES:

Anchorage Office
University Plaza
949 East 36th Avenue
Anchorage, Alaska 99508-4399
907.271.4170

Boise Office
800 Park Boulevard, Suite 220
Boise, Idaho 83712-7743
208.334.1990

Portland Office
520 Southwest Sixth Avenue
Portland, Oregon 97204-1596
503.326.2561

Spokane Office
Farm Credit Bank Building
Eighth Floor East
West 601 First Avenue
Spokane, Washingon 99204-0317
509.353.2510

Appendix B:
Area Trustees for
Bankruptcy Sales

REGION 1

(Maine, Massachusetts, New Hampshire,
Rhode Island)
United States Trustee
10 Causeway St., Rm. 472
Boston, MA 02222-1184
(Check your local newspaper.)

REGION 2

(Connecticut, New York, Vermont)
United States Trustee
80 Broad St., 3rd Floor
New York, NY 10004-1408
212/668-2200

REGION 3

(Delaware, New Jersey, Pennsylvania)
United States Trustee
601 Walnut St., Rm. 950W
Philadelphia, PA 19106
215/597-4411

REGION 4

(Washington, D.C., Maryland, North
Carolina, South Carolina, Virginia, West
Virginia)
United States Trustee
1201 Main St., Rm. 2440
Columbia, SC 29201
803/765-5599

REGION 5

(Louisiana, Mississippi)
United States Trustee
400 Poydras St., Ste. 2110
New Orleans, LA 70130
504/589-4018

REGION 6

(Northern and Eastern Texas)
United States Trustee
U.S. Courthouse, Rm. 9C60
1100 Commerce St.
Dallas, TX 75242
214/767-8967

REGION 7

(Southern and Western Texas)
United States Trustee
440 Louisiana St., Ste. 2500
Houston, TX 77002
713/718-4650

REGION 8

(Kentucky, Tennessee)
United States Trustee
200 Jefferson Ave., Ste. 400
Memphis, TN 38103
901/544-3251

REGION 9

(Michigan, Ohio)
United States Trustee
113 St. Clair Ave., NE, Ste. 200
Cleveland, OH 44114
216/522-7800

REGION 10

(Indiana, Central and Southern Illinois)
United States Trustee
101 West Ohio St., Rm. 1000
Indianapolis, IN 46204
317/226-6101

REGION 11

(Wisconsin, Northern Illinois)
United States Trustee
227 West Monroe St.
Chicago, IL 60606

REGION 12

(Iowa, Minnesota, North Dakota, South
Dakota)
United States Trustee
425 Second St., SE, Rm. 675
Cedar Rapids, IA 52401
319/364-2211

REGION 13

(Arkansas, Nebraska, Mississippi)
500 S. Broadway, Ste. 205
Little Rock, AR 72201
816/824-7357

REGION 14

(Arizona)
United States Trustee
320 North Central Ave., Rm. 100
Phoenix, AZ 85004
602/379-3092

REGION 15

(Southern California, Hawaii, Guam,
Northern Mariana Islands)
United States Trustee
101 West Broadway, Ste. 440
San Diego, CA 92101
619/557-5013

REGION 16

(Central California)
United States Trustee
Federal Bldg., Rm. 800
221 N. Figueroa
Los Angeles, CA 90012
213/894-6811

REGION 17

(Eastern and Northern California, Nevada)
United States Trustee
250 Montgomery St. Suite 910
San Francisco, CA 94104
415/705-3300

REGION 18

(Idaho, Montana, Oregon, Washington)
United States Trustee
1200 6th Ave., Rm. 600
Seattle, WA 98101
206/553-2000

REGION 19

(Colorado, Utah, Wyoming)
United States Trustee
721 19th St., Ste. 408
Denver, CO 80202
303/844-5188

REGION 20

(Kansas, New Mexico, Oklahoma)
United States Trustee
401 N. Market St., Rm. 180
Wichita, KS 67202
316/269-6637

REGION 21

(Alabama, Florida, Georgia, Puerto Rico,
Virgin Islands)
United States Trustee
75 Spring St. SW, Ste. 362
Atlanta, GA 30303
404/331-4437

Appendix C: IRS Regional and State Offices

CENTRAL REGION
(IN, KY, MI, OH, WV)
Box 1699
Cincinnnati, OH 45201
513.684.2514 Hotline

MID-ATLANTIC REGION
(DE, DC, MD, NJ, PA, VA)
1601 Market St.
Philadelphia, PA 19103
215.656.7940
215.597.4030 Hotline

MID-WEST REGION
(IL, MN, MO, MT, NE, ND, SD, WI, IA)
Gateway IV Bldg.
300 South Riverside Plaza
Chicago, IL 60606-6683
312.886.5600

NORTH-ATLANTIC REGION
(CT, ME, MA, NH, NY, RI, VT)
Box 269, Church Street Station
New York, NY 10008
212.264.7061
718-488-2717 Hotline

SOUTHEAST REGION
(AL, AR, FL, GA, LA, MS, NC, SC, TN)
Box 926, Stop 100-R
Atlanta, GA 30370
404.331.6048
800.829.9348 Hotline

SOUTHWEST REGION
(AZ, CO, KS, NM, OK, TX, UT, WY)
4050 Alpha Road
Dallas, TX 75244-4203
214.308.7000

WESTERN REGION
(AK, CA, HI, ID, NV, OR, WA)
Box 420889
San Francisco, CA 94142-0889
415.556.3300
415.556.5021 Hotline

AUCTION ADDRESSES

ALABAMA
IRS
Special Procedures Function
500 22nd St., Stop 216
Birmingham, AL 35233
205.731.1251

ALASKA
IRS
Group Manager
949 East 36th St.
Anchorage, AK 99508
(Alaska residents only)
907.271.6200

ARIZONA
IRS
Special Procedures Function
2120 N.Central Ave.
Phoenix, AZ 85004
602.207.8500

ARKANSAS
IRS
Special Procedures Function
ATTN: Bidder's List
700 West Capitol St.
Little Rock, AR 72202
501.324.5338

CALIFORNIA
IRS
Special Procedures Function
2400 Avila Road
Laguna Niguel, CA 92607-0227
Los Angeles   213.894.4120
Sacramento   916.974.5923
San Francisco   510.637.2370
San Jose   408.494.8500

COLORADO
Denver
303.446.1431

DELAWARE
IRS
Special Procedures Function
409 Silverside Road
Wilmington, DE 19809
302.791.4534

DISTRICT OF COLUMBIA
410.962.9401

FLORIDA
IRS
Box 17167, Stop 5720
Fort Lauderdale, FL 33318
305.423.7769

IRS
Box 35045, Stop 5750
Jacksonville, FL 32202
904.279.1656 Hotline

GEORGIA
401 Peachtree St.
Atlanta, GA 30365
800.829.9348

HAWAII
Honolulu
808.541.1104

IDAHO
IRS
Special Procedures Function
550 West Fort Street
Boise, ID 83724
208.334.1273

ILLINOIS
IRS
ATTN: Automation Unit, DPN-17-5
Box 1112
Chicago, IL 60690

INDIANA
Indianapolis
317.226.5946
Gary   219.736.4308
Evansville   812.471.6605

IOWA
IRS

Special Procedures
Function
Box 313
Des Moines, Iowa 50302
515.284.4300

KANSAS
IRS
Special Procedures
Function
412 South Main Stret
Witchita, KS 67202

KENTUCKY
IRS
Chief, Collection Field
Function
Box 1054, Stop 520
Louisville, KY 40201
502.582.5334

LOUISIANA
600 S. Maestri Place
Stop 6
New Orleans, LA 70130
504.589.2875

MARYLAND
Baltimore
410.962.9401

MICHIGAN
IRS
Box 330500, Stop 6
Detroit, MI 48322
313.226.7157

MINNESOTA
St. Paul
612.290.4042

MISSISSIPPI
IRS
Special Procedures
Function
100 West Capitol St. Ste. 504
Jackson, MS 39269
601.965.4474

MISSOURI
IRS
Special Procedures
Function
Box 1457
St. Louis, MO 63188

MONTANA
IRS
Special Procedures
Function
Drawer 10016
Helena, MT 59626

NEBRASKA
IRS

Special Procedures Function
Box 622
Omaha, NE 68101
402.221.3578
402.221.3492 Hotline

NEW JERSEY
IRS
Special Procedures Function
Box 166
Newark, NJ 07101
201.645.3829

NEW MEXICO
Albuquerque
505.837.5792

NEVADA
Las Vegas
702.455.1058

NEW YORK
Brooklyn
718.488.2717
Manhattan
212.264.1681

NORTH CAROLINA
Greensboro
919.378-2073

NORTH DAKOTA
IRS
Special Procedures Function
Box 2461
Fargo, ND 58108
701.250.4235

OHIO
Cleveland
216.522.7902/2100
513.684.2514

OKLAHOMA
IRS
Special Procedures Function
200 N.W. 4th St.
Oklahoma City, OK 73102

OREGON
Portland
503.326.7840

PENNSYLVANIA
IRS
Special Procedures Function
Box 12051
Philadelphia, PA 19105
215.597.4207

PENNSYLVANIA
IRS
SPF Advisory Unit
Chamber of Commerce
Building

411 7th Ave., 5th Floor
Pittsburgh, PA 15219

SOUTH CAROLINA
1835 Assembly St.
Columbia, SC 29201
803.765.5701

SOUTH DAKOTA
IRS
Special Procedures Function
Box 370
Aberdeen, SD 57401
605.226.7210

TENNESSEE
801 Broadway
Nashville, TN 37203
615.736.5731

TEXAS
IRS
Special Procedures Function
1100 Commerce Street
Dallas, TX 75242

TEXAS
IRS
Special Procedures Function
1919 Smith Street
Houston, TX 77002-8049

TEXAS
Austin
512.499.5241

VIRGINIA
IRS
Special Procedures Function
Box 10025
Richmond, VA 23240
804.771.2811

WEST VIRGINIA
IRS
ATTNL Brendell Cramer
Box 1138
Parkersburg, WV 26102
304.420.6631/6970

WASHINGTON
Seattle
206.220.5461

WISCONSIN
Milwaukee
414.297.1292

WYOMING
IRS
Special Procedures Function
308 21st Street
Cheyenne, WY 82001
307.772.2641

Appendix D: VA Offices

ALABAMA
Regional Office:
345 Perry Hill Rd.
Montgomery, AL 36109
(334) 213-3420 Prop. Mgmt.

ALASKA
Regional Office:
2925 DeBarr Rd.
Anchorage, AK 99508-2829
907-257-4745 Prop. Mgmt.

ARIZONA
Regional Office:
3225 N. Central Ave.
Phoenix, AZ 85012
602-640-4748 Prop. Mgmt.

ARKANSAS
Regional Office:
Bldg. 65 Ft. Roots
P.O. Box 1280
North Little Rock, AR 72115
501-370-3763 Prop. Mgmt.

CALIFORNIA
Regional Offices:
Federal Bldg. 11000 Wilshire
Blvd
Los Angeles, CA 90024
310-235-7838 ext. 6096 Prop.
Mgmt.
(Counties of Inyo, Kern, Los Angeles,
Orange, San Bernadino, Santa Barbara,
San Luis Obispo, Ventura)

1301 Clay St. Rm. 1300 North
Oakland, CA 94612
510-637-1365 Prop. Mgmt.
(Counties of Alpine, Lassen, Modoc, and
Mono are served by the Reno, NV office)

COLORADO & WYOMING
Regional Office
44 Union Blvd. P.O. Box 25126
Denver, CO 80225
303-980-2870 Prop. Mgmt.

CONNECTICUT
Regional Office:
450 Main St.
Hartford, CT 06103
203-278-3230

DELAWARE
Regional Office:
1601 Kirkwood Hwy.
Wilmington, DE 19805
302-998-0191 (local)

DISTRICT OF COLUMBIA
Regional Office:
1120 Vermont Ave. N.W.
Washington, D.C. 20421

202-418-4270 Prop. Mgmt.

FLORIDA
Regional Office:
144 1st Ave S.
St. Petersburg, FL 33701
813-898-2121 (local)

GEORGIA
Regional Office:
730 Peachtree ST. NE
Atlanta, GA 30365
404-347-3474 Prop. Mgmt.

HAWAII
Regional Office:
P.O. Box 50188
300 Ala Moana Blvd.
Honolulu, HI 96850-001
808-566-1475 Prop. Mgmt.

IDAHO
Regional Office:
805 W. Franklin St.
Boise, ID 83702
208-334-1010 (local)

ILLINOIS
Regional Office:
536 S. Clark St. P.O. Box 8136
Chicago, IL 60680
708-663-5510 (local)

INDIANA
Regional Office:
575 N. Pennsylvania St.
Indianapolis, IN 46202
317-226-7801 Prop. Mgmt.

IOWA
Regional Office:
210 Walnut St.
Des Moines, IA 50309
515-284-4241 Prop. Mgmt.

KANSAS
Regional Office:
5500 E. Kellogg
Wichita, KS 67211
316-688-6858 Prop. Mgmt.

KENTUCKY
Regional Office:
545 S. Third St.
Louisville, KY 40202
502-582-5866 Prop. Mgmt.

LOUISIANA
Regional Office:
701 Loyola Ave.
New Orleans, LA 70113
504-589-6458 Prop. Mgmt.

MAINE
Regional Office:
Route 17 East
Togus, ME 04330
207-623-8000 Prop. Mgmt.

MARYLAND
Regional Office:
31 Hopkins Plaza Federal Bldg.
Baltimore, MD 21201
410-962-7874 Prop. Mgmt.
(Counties of Montgomery, Prince Georges
served by D.C. office)

MASSACHUSETTS
Regional Office:
JFK Federal Bldg. Government
Center
Boston, MA 02203
617-232-9500 (local)
(Towns of Fall River and New Bedford,
counties of Barnstable, Dukes, Nantucket,
Bristol, part of Plymouth served by
Providence, RI office)

MICHIGAN
Regional Office:
Patrick V. McNamara Federal
Bldg.
477 Michigan Ave.
Detroit, MI 48226
313-226-4200 Prop. Mgmt.

MINNESOTA
Regional Office:
Bishop Henry Whipple Federal
Bldg.
1 Federal Dr., Fort Snelling
St. Paul. MN 55111
612-725-3870 Prop. Mgmt.
800-827-0633 Hotline
(Counties of Becker, Beltrami, Clay,
Clearwater, Kittson, Lake of the Woods,
Mahnomen, Marshall, Norman, Otter Trail,
Pennington, Polk, Red Lake, Roseau, and
Wilkin served by Fargo, ND office)

MISSISSIPPI
Regional Office:
100 W. Capitol St.
Jackson, MS 39269
601-965-4975 Prop. Mgmt.

MISSOURI
Regional Office:
400 S. 18th St.
St. Louis, MO 63103
314-589-9865 Prop. Mgmt.

MONTANA
Regional Office:
Fort Harrison, MT 59636
406-444-4514

NEBRASKA
Regional Office:
5631 S. 48 th St.
Lincoln, NE 68516
402-437-5031 Prop. Mgmt.

NEVADA

Regional Office:
1201 Terminal Way
Reno, NV 89520
602-640-4748

NEW JERSEY
Regional Office:
20 Washington Place
Newark, NJ 07102
201-645-3608 Prop. Mgmt.

NEW MEXICO
Regional Office:
Dennis Chavez Federal Bldg.
500 Gold Ave. S.W.
Albuquerque, NM 87102
505-766-1026 Prop. Mgmt.

NEW YORK
Regional Offices:
Federal Bldg. 111 W, Huron St.
Buffalo, NY 14202
716-846-5293 Prop. Mgmt.
(Serves counties not served by New York City Regional Office)

252 Seventh Ave. At 24th St.
NYC, NY 10001
212-620-6330 (voice mail)
(Serves counties of Albany, Bronx, Clinton, Columbia, Delaware, Dutchess, Essex, Franklin, Fulton, Greene, Hamilton, King, Montgomery, Nassau, New York, Orange, Otsego, Putnam, Queens, Rensselaer, Richmond, Rockland, Saratoga, Schenectady, Schoharie, Suffolk, Sullivan, Ulster, Warren, Washington, Westchester)

NORTH CAROLINA
Regional Office:
Federal Bldg. 251 N. Main St.
Winston-Salem, NC 27155
910-748-1800 Prop. Mgmt.

NORTH DAKOTA
Regional Office:
2101 Elm St.
Fargo, ND 58102
800-827-0633 Prop. Mgmt.

OHIO
Regional Office:
Anthony J. Celebrazze Fed. Bldg.
1240 E. Ninth St.
Cleveland, OH 44199
800-827-1000

OKLAHOMA
Regional Office:
Federal Bldg. 25 S. Main St.
Muskogee, OK 74401
918-687-2161 Prop. Mgmt.

OREGON
Regional Office:
Federal Bldg. 1220 S.W. 3rd Ave.
Portland, OR 97204
503-326-2484 Prop. Mgmt.

PENNSYLVANIA
Regional Offices:
P.O. Box 8079, 5000 Wissahicken Ave.
Philadelphia, PA 19101
215-951-5508 (local)
(Serves counties of Adams, Berks, Bradford, Bucks, Cameron, Carbon, Centre, Chester, Clinton, Columbia, Cumberland, Dauphin, Delaware, Franklin, Juniata, Lackawanna, Lancaster, Lebanon, Lehigh, Luzerne, Lycoming, Mifflin, Monroe. Montgomery, Montour, Northampton, Northumberland, Perry, Philadelphia, Pike, Potter, Schuylkill, Snyder, Sullivan, Susquehanna, Tioga, Union, Wayne, Wyoming, York)

1000 Liberty Ave.
Pittsburgh, PA 15222
412-281-4233 (local)

PHILLIPPINES
Regional Office:
1131 Roxas Blvd.
Manilla 1000
521-7521 (local)

PUERTO RICO
Regional Office:
U.S. Courthouse and Federal Bldg.
Carlos E. Chardon St.
Hato Rey, GPO Box 4867
San Juan, PR 00936
766-5141 (local)

RHODE ISLAND
380 Westminster Mall
Providence, RI 02903
603-666-7443 Prop. Mgmt.

SOUTH CAROLINA
Regional Office:
1801 Assembly St.
Columbia, SC 29201
803-765-5154 Prop. Mgmt.

SOUTH DAKOTA
Regional Office:
P.O. Box 5046
2501 W. 22nd St.
Sioux Falls, SD 57117
800-827-0611 Prop. Mgmt.

TENNESSEE
Regional Office:
110 9th Ave. South
Nashville, TN 37203
615-736-5241 (local)

TEXAS
Regional Offices:
8900 Lakes at 610 Dr.
Houston, Texas 77054
713-791-1444

(Serves counties of Angelina, Aransas, Atacosa, Austin, Bandera, Bee, Bexar, Blanco, Brazoria, Brewster, Brooks, Caldwell, Calhoun, Cameron, Chambers, Colorado, Comal, Crockett, DeWitt, Dimitt, Duval,Edwards, Fort Bend, Frio, Galveston, Gillespie, Goliad, Gonzalez, Grimes, Guadalupe, Hardin, Harris, Hays, Hidalgo, Houston, Jackson, Jasper, Jefferson., Jim Hogg, Jim Wells, Karnes, Kendall, Kenedy, Kerr, Kimble, Kinney, Kleberg, LaSalle, Lavaca, Liberty, Live Oak, McColluch, McMullen, Mason, Matagorda, Maverick, Medina, Menard, Montgomery, Nacogdoches, Newton, Nueces, Orange, Pecos, Polk, Real, Refugio, Sabine, San Augustine, San Jacinto, San Patricio, Schleicher, Shelby, Starr, Sutton, Terrell. Trinity, Tyler, Uvalde, Val Verde, Victoria, Walker, Waller, Washington, Webb, Wharton, Willacy, Wilson, Zapata, Zavala)

1400 N. Valley Mills Dr.
Waco, TX 76799
817-757-6869 Property Management
(Serves rest of the state; Bowie County served by Little Rock, AR Regional Office)

UTAH
Regional Office:
P.O. Box 11500,
Federal Bldg.
125 S. State St.
Salt Lake City, UT 84147
801-524-6750 Prop. Mgmt.

VERMONT
Regional Office:
N. Hartland Rd.
White River Junction, VT 05009
603-666-7525 Prop. Mgmt.

VIRGINIA
Regional Office:
210 Franklin Rd. SW
Roanoke, VA 24011
800-827-1000 Prop. Mgmt.
(N. Virginia counties of Arlington and Fairfax, Cities of Alexandria and Fairfax, Falls Church served by Wahington, D.C. Regional Office)

WASHINGTON
Regional Office:
Federal Bldg. 915 2nd Ave.
Seattle, WA 98121
206-220-6166 Prop. Mgmt.

WEST VIRGINIA
Regional Office:
640 Fourth Ave.
Huntington, WV 25701
304-529-5046 Prop. Mgmt.

WISCONSIN
V.A. Regional Office
Bldg. 6 Room 266
Milwaukee, WI 53295
414-383-8680 (local)

WYOMING
Regional Office:
2360 E. Perdhing Blvd.
Cheyenne, WY 82001
307-980-2908 Prop. Mgmt.

Appendix E:
State Surplus Property Offices

ALABAMA
Alabama State Agency for
Surplus Property Assistance
Economic and County
Affairs Dept.
Box 210487
Montgomery, AL 36121
205/277-5866

ALASKA
Alaska Surplus Property
Service
2400 Viking Dr.
Anchorage, AK 99501
907/465-2172

ARIZONA
Surplus Management Office
General Services Division
1537 West Jackson
Phoenix, AZ 85007
602/542-5701

ARKANSAS
Agency for Federal Surplus
Property
Dept. of Education
8700 Remount Rd.
North Little Rock, AR 72118
501/835-3111

CALIFORNIA
Agency for Surplus Property
Office of Real Estate &
Design
400 R. St. Ste. 5000
Sacramento, CA 95814
916/322-4067

COLORADO
Colorado Surplus Property
Agency
Dept. of Corrections
4200 Garfield St.
Denver, CO 80216-6517
303/321-4012

CONNECTICUT
Surplus Property Program
Dept. of Administrative
Services
60 State St.
Wethersford, CT 06129-0170
203/566-7018

DELAWARE
Delaware Division of
Purchasing
Dept. of Administrative
Services
Box 299
Delaware City, DE 19706
302/834-7081

DISTRICT OF COLUMBIA
Material Management
Surplus
Acquisition Services
Dept. of Administrative
Services
2000 Adams Place, NE
Washington, DC 20017
202/576-6472

FLORIDA
Florida Division of Surplus
Properties
Dept. of General Services
813-A Lakebradford Rd.
Tallahassee, FL 32304
904/488-3524

GEORGIA
Agency for Surplus Properties
Purchasing Division
Dept. of Administrative
Services
1050 Murphy Ave. SW,
Building 1A
Atlanta, GA 30310
404/756-4800

GUAM
Surplus Property Section
Division of Personnel
Dept. of Administration
Box 884
Agana, Guam 96910
011/671-475-1101

HAWAII
Surplus Property Branch
Purchasing and Supply Division
Dept. of General Services
1151 Punchbowl St. Rm 416
Honolulu, HI 96813
808/831-6757

IDAHO
Bureau of Surplus Property
General Services Division
Dept. of Administration
3204 East Amity
Boise, ID 83705

INDIANA
Indiana State Agency for
Federal Surplus Property
1401 N. Milburn St.
Indianapolis, IN 46202
317/232-1365

IOWA
Surplus Property Section
Purchasing & Management
Division
Dept. of General Services
Hoover State Office Bldg.,
Level A
Des Moines, IA 50319
515/281-3089/5856

Dept. of Natural Resources
Wallace State Office Bldg.
Des Moines, IA 50319
515/281-5145

LOUISIANA
Louisiana Surplus Property
Agency
Procurement Office
1059 Brickyard Ln.
Baton Rouge, LA 70802
504/342-6849

ILLINOIS
Property Control Division
Bureau Of Property
Management
Dept. Of Central
Management Services
3550 Great Northern St.
Springfield, IL 62707
(217) 785-6903

KANSAS
Kansas State Surplus
Property
Box 19226
Topeka, KS 66619-0226
913/296-2334

KENTUCKY
Surplus & Personal Property
Management Section
Division Of Purchases
383 State Street Capitol
Annex
Frankfort, KY 40601
502/564-4510

MAINE
Office of Surplus Property
State House Station 95
Augusta, ME 04333
207/289-5750

MASSACHUSETTS
Massachusetts State
Agency for Federal Surplus
Property
Procurement & General
Services Dept.
One Ashburton Place
Room 1017
Boston, MA 02108
617) 727-7500/2920

MISSISSIPPI
Bureau of Surplus Property
Box 5778
Whitfield Road
Jackson, MS 39288-5778
601/939-2050

MISSOURI
Surplus Property Office
117 North Riverside Drive
Jefferson City, MO 65102
314/751-3415

MARYLAND
State Agency for Surplus
Property
Services & Logistics Division
General Services Dept.
8037 Brock Bridge Rd., Box
1039
Jessuup, MD 20794
410/799-0440

MICHIGAN
Sstate Surplus Property
Office of Fed. Prop.
Assistance
Office Services Division
Dept. of Management and
Budget
3353 N. Martin Luther King
Blvd.
Lansing, MI 48913
517/335-8444

MINNESOTA
Surplus Operations Office
5420 Highway 8
New Brighton, MN 55112
612/296-5177
800/296-1056 (in MN)

MONTANA
Property & Supply Bureau
Administration Dept.
155 Mitchell Bldg.
Helena, MT 59620
406/444-4514

NEBRASKA
Office of Administrative
Services
Material Division, Surplus
Property
Box 94910
Lincoln, NE 68509
402/479-4890

NEW HAMPSHIRE
Office of Surplus Property
78 Regional Drive
Building 3
Concord, NH 03301
603/271-2126

NEW MEXICO
Agency for Surplus Property
General Services Dept.
1990 Siringo Rd.
Santa Fe, NM 87505
505/827-4603

NEVADA
Surplus Property Office
Nevada State Purchasing
Division
General Services Dept.
209 E. Musser St.
Carson City, NV 89710
702/687-4070

NEW JERSEY
New Jersey Real Property
Management
Purchase & Property
Distribution Center
CN234
Trenton, NJ 08625-0234
609/530-3300

NEW YORK
Bureau of Land
Management
Office of General Services,
Rm. 2689
Empire State Plaza, Corning
Tower
Albany, NY 12242
518/474-2195

NORTH CAROLINA
State Surplus Properties
Box 33900
Raeligh, NC 27636
919/733-3889

OHIO
State & Federal Surplus
Property
(Call your local Sheriff's Department)

OREGON
Dept. of Surplus Property
1655 Salem Industrial Dr., NE
Salem, OR 97310
503/378-4714

NORTH DAKOTA
Surplus Property Office
Box 7293
Bismarck, ND 58507
701/328-2273

OKLAHOMA
State Agency for Surplus
Property
Office of Public Affairs
Box 11355
Oklahoma City, OK 73136
405/425-2700

PENNSYLVANIA
Bureau of Supplies & Surplus
General Services Dept.
2221 Forestor St.
Harrisburg, PA 17105
717/787-4083

PUERTO RICO
Surplus Property Program
Div. of Purchasing Services
& Supply
General Services
Admdinistration
Box 7428
Barrio Obrero Station
San Turce, PR 00916
809/721-7370

SOUTH DAKOTA
Bureau of Administration
State Property Management
104 S. Garfield Ave.
Pierre, SD 57501
605/773-4935

TENNESSEE
Dept. of General Services
Prop. Utilization Division
6500 Centennial Boulevard
Nashville, TN 37209
615/741-1711

UTAH
Utah State Surplus Property
522 South 700 West Street
Salt Lake City, UT 84104
801/533-5885

RHODE ISLAND
State Agency for Surplus
Property
Division of Purchases
Dept. of Administration
One Capitol Hill
Providence, RI 02908
401/277-2321

SOUTH CAROLINA
Surplus Property
Management
General Services Division
Budget & Control Board
1441 Boston Ave.
Columbia, SC 29170-2194
803/822-5490

TEXAS
General Services
Commission
2103 Ackerman Rd., Box
8120
San Antonio, TX 78208
210/661-2381

VERMONT
Central Surplus Property
Agency
RD 2 Box 520
Montpelier, VT 05602
802/828-3394

VIRGINIA
State Surplus Property
Box 1199
Richmond, VA 23209
804/236-3666

WASHINGTON
Commodity Redistribution
Division
General Administration
Dept.
2805 C Street, SW
Building 5, Door 49
Auburn, WA 98001
206/931-3931

WISCONSIN
Federal Surplus Property
Program
Administration Dept.
Box 7880
Madison, WI 53707-7880
608/266-8024

SAMOA
Office of Procurement
Agency for Surplus Property
Administration Services
Dept.
Pago Pago, AS 96799
011/684-633-4158

VIRGIN ISLANDS
Agency for Surplus Property
Property & Procurement
Division
Division of Property &
Printing
Bldg. One Subbage
St. Thomas, VI 00802
809/774-0828

WEST VIRGINIA
State Agency for Surplus
Property
Dept. of Finance &
Administration
2700 Charles Ave.
Dunbar, WV 25064
304/766-2626

WYOMING
Surplus Property
2045 Westland Rd.
Cheyenne, WY 82002

Appendix F: RECD State Offices

ALABAMA
Horace Horn
Sterling Center, Suite 601
4121 Carmichael Rd .
Montgomery, AL 36106-3683
(205) 279-3400

ALASKA
Ernest Brannon
634 S. Bailey, Suite 103
Palmer, AK 99645
(907) 745-2176

ARIZONA
Alan Stephens
3003 North Central Ave,
Suite 900
Phoenix, AZ 85012
(602) 280-8755

ARKANSAS
700 W. Capitol, Rm. 5411
Little Rock, AR 72201-3225
(501) 324-6281

CALIFORNIA
Michael Reyna
194 West Main St. Suite F
Woodland, CA 95695-2915
(916) 668-2000

COLORADO
Ruth Rodriguez
655 Parfet St., Rm E-100
Lakewood, CO 80215
(303) 236-2801

DELAWARE-MARYLAND
John Walls
4611 So. Dupont Hwy.
P.O. Box 400
Camden, DE 19934-9998
(302) 697-4300

FLORIDA
Jan Shadburn
4440 NW 25th Pl.
P.O. Box 147010
Gainesville, FL 32614-7010
(904) 338-3400

GEORGIA
Laura Jean Meadows
Stephens Federal Building
355 E. Hancock Ave.
Athens, GA 30601-2768
(706) 546-2173

HAWAII
Francis Blanco
Federal Bldg., Rm 311
154 Waianuenue Avenue
Hilo, HI 96720
(808) 933-3000

IDAHO
Loren Nelson
3232 Elder Street
Boise, ID 83705
(208) 334- 1301

ILLINOIS
Wallace Furrow
Illini Plaza, Suite 103
1817 South Neil Street
Champaign, IL 61820
(217) 398-5235

INDIANA
John Thompson
5975 Lakeside Blvd.
Indianapolis, IN 46278
(317) 290-3100

IOWA
Ellen Huntoon
Federal Building, Rm 873
210 Walnut Street
Des Moines, IA 50309
(515) 284-4663

KANSAS
Bill Kirk
P.O. Box 4653
Topeka, KS 66604-0653
(913) 271-2700

KENTUCKY
Tom Fern
771 Corporate Dr.
Suite 200
Lexington, KY 40503
(606) 224-7300

LOUISIANA
Austin Cormier
3727 Government Street
Alexandria, LA 71302
(318) 473-7920

MAINE
Seth Bradstreet
444 Stillwater Avenue,
Suite 2
P.O. Box 405
Bangor, ME 04402-0405
(207) 990-9106

MASS/RHODE ISLAND/CT
William Bradley
451 West Street
Amherst, MA 01002
(413) 253-4300

MICHIGAN
Donald Hare
3001 Coolidge Rd., Suite 200
East Lansing, MI 48823
(517) 337-6635

MINNESOTA
Janice Daley
410 Farm Credit Service
Bldg.
375 Jackson Street
St. Paul, MN 55101
(612) 290-3842

MISSISSIPPI
George E. Irvin
Federal Building, Rm 831
100 W. Capitol Street
Jackson, MS 39269
(601) 965-4316

MISSOURI
William Shay (Acting)
601 Business Loop 70 West
Parkade Center, Suite 235
Columbia, MO 65203
(314) 876-0976

MONTANA
Anthony Preite
900 Technology Blvd., Suite B
PO Box 850
Bozeman, MT 59771
(406) 585-2515

NEBRASKA
Stanley Foster
Federal Bldg., Rm 308
100 Centennial Mall N
Lincoln, NE 68508
(402) 437-5551

NEW JERSEY
Ernest Grunow
Tarnsfield Plaza, Suite 22
1016 Woodlane Rd.
Mt. Holly, NJ 08060
(609) 265-3600

NEW MEXICO
Steven Anaya
600 Jefferson St. N.E. Rm. 255
Albuquerque, NM 87109
(505) 761-4950
(505) 761-4977 fax

NEW YORK
James Bay
The Galleries of Syracuse
441 S. Salina Street
Syracuse, NY 13202
(315) 477-6400

NORTH CAROLINA
James Kearney
4405 Bland Road, Suite 260
Raleigh, NC 27609
(919) 790-2731

NORTH DAKOTA
Charles Mertens
Federal Building, Rm 208
3rd & Rosser, PO Box 1737
Bismarck, ND 58502
(701) 250-4781

OHIO
Linda Page
Federal Building, Rm 507
200 North High Street
Columbus, OH 43215
(614) 469-5606

OKLAHOMA
Charles Rainbolt
USDA Agricultural Center
Stillwater, OK 74074
(405) 742-1000

OREGON
Scott Duff
101 SW Main St.
Suite 1410
Portland, OR 97204-2333
(503) 414-3300

PENNSYLVANIA
Cheryl Cook
1 Credit Union Place,
Suite 330
Harrisburg, PA 17110-2996
(717) 782-4476

SOUTH CAROLINA
Bernie Wright
Strom Thurmond Federal
Bldg.
1835 Assembly Street,
Rm 1007
Columbia, SC 29201
(803) 765-5163

SOUTH DAKOTA
Dallas Tonsager
Federal Building, Rm 308
200 4th Street SW
Huron, SD 57350
(605) 352-1100

TENNESSEE
David Seivers
3322 West End Ave.,
Suite 300
Nashville, TN 37203-1071
(615) 783-1308

TEXAS
George Ellis, M. J. Pena
Federal Building, Suite 102
101 South Main
Temple, TX 76501
(817) 774-1301

NEVADA
Sarah Mersereau
1390 South Curry St.
Carson City, NV 89703-5405
(702) 887-1222

VERMONT/NEW HAMPSHIRE/VI
Roberta Harold
City Center, 3rd Floor
89 Main St.
Montpelier, VT 05602
(802) 828-6001

VIRGINIA
Lloyd A. Jones
Culpeper Building, Suite 238
1606 Santa Rosa Road
Richmond, VA 23229
(804) 287-1550

WASHINGTON
George Aldaya
Federal Building, Rm 319
301 Yakima St., PO Box 2427
Wenatchee, WA 98807
(509) 664-0240

WEST VIRGINIA
Robert Lewis Federal Bldg.
Rm. 320
75 High Street
Morgantown, WV 26505
(304) 291-4791

WISCONSIN
Bryce Luchterhand
4949 Kirschling Crt.
Stevens Point, WI 54481
(715) 345-7625

WYOMING
Derrel L. Carruth
Federal Building, Rm 1005
P.O. Box 820
Casper, WY 82602
(307) 261-5271

Bibliography

BOOKS

Achenbach, George. *Goldmining in Foreclosure Properties.* Third Edition. John Wiley and Sons, 1994.

Allen, Robert G. *Nothing Down for the 90s.* Simon and Schuster, 1990.

Barash, Samuel. *Standard Real Estate Appraising Manual.* Prentice Hall.

Beck, Sue. *How to Buy Your Home . . . and Do It Right.* Dearborn Financial Publishing, Inc., 1993.

Bergman, Bruce J. *Bergman on New York Mortgage Foreclosures.* Bender, 1990.

Blankenship, Frank. *The Prentice Hall Real Estate Investor's Encyclopedia.* Prentice Hall.

Bockl, George. *How to Use Leverage to Make Money in Local Real Estate.* Prentice Hall.

Boroson, Warren and Austin, Ken. *The Home Buyer's Inspection Guide.* John Wiley and Sons, 1993.

Campbell, William A. *Property Tax Lien Foreclosure Forms & Procedures.* Institute Government, 1992.

Caron, Denis R. *Connecticut Foreclosure Supplement.* Connecticut Law Tribunal, 1991.

Coffey, Kendall. *Florida Foreclosures: Remedies, Defenses, & Lender Liability.* Butterworth Legal Publishers, 1992.

Cummings, Jack. *Complete Guide to Real Estate Financing.* Prentice Hall.

Cummings, Jack. *Real Estate Financing Manual: A Guide to Money Making Strategies.* Prentice Hall.

Dasso, Jerome and Ring, Alfred A. *Real Estate Principles and Practices,* 11th edition. Prentice Hall, 1989.

Detweiler, Gerri. *The Ultimate Credit Handbook.* Plume Books, 1993.

Eastgate, Robert. *Master Guide to Creative Financing of Real Estate Investments.* Prentice Hall.

Friedman, Jack P.; Harris, Jack C. *Keys to Buying a Foreclosed Home.* Barron, 1992.

Glazer, Gerald S.; Porter, Jack N. *Foreclosed Real Estate: Your Profit Opportunity.* Spencer Press, 1992.

Glink, Ilyce R. *100 Questions Every First-Time Home Buyer Should Ask.* Times Books-Random House, 1994.

Gross, Jerome. *New Encyclopedia of Real Estate Forms.* Prentice Hall.

Harwood, Bruce. *Real Estate: An Introduction to the Profession,* 4th ed. Reston Publishing Company, 1986.

Hoffman, Tony. *How to Negotiate Successfully in Real Estate.* Simon and Schuster, 1984.

Hootman, Marcia J.; Garner, Cindy; Garner, Alan-Editor. *Cash in on Tax Lien Certificates: Earn Up to 50 Percent or Buy Real Estate for Pennies on the Dollar.* Newport House, 1990.

Jorgensen, R.H. *How to Find Hidden Wealth in Local Real Estate.* Prentice Hall.

Kiplinger's Buying & Selling a Home. Kiplinger Books, 1990.

Kollen, Melissa S. *Buying Real Estate Foreclosures.* McGraw Hill, 1992.

Lohmar, Ceil. *For Sale By Owner.* Chicago: Probus Publishing Company, 1990.

Locke, William H., Jr.; Novak, Ralph M., Jr. *Texas Foreclosure Manual.* State Bar of Texas, 1991.

Lucier, Thomas J. *How to Make Money Buying Pre-Foreclosure Properties Before They Hit the County Courthouse Steps.* Real Estate Publications, 1993.

McLean, Andrew James. *Buying Real Estate for Pennies on the Dollar: How to Make a Fortune in Foreclosures.* Contemporary Books, 1992.

Miller, Peter G. *Buy Your First Home Now.* Harper & Row Publishers, 1990.

Miller, Peter G. and Bregman, Dougls M. *Successful Real Estate Negotiation, Revised Edition.* Harper Perennial, 1994.

Morrison, James W. *The Complete Energy Saving Handbook for Homeowners.* Harper & Row, 1979.

Moses, Phillip. *How to Make Big Money Acquiring and Renovating Older Neglected Real Estate.* Prentice Hall.

Nessen, Robert L. *The Real Estate Book*, rev. ed. Little, Brown and Company, 1983.

Percelay, Bruce A. and Arnold, Peter. *Packaging Your Home for Profit.* Little, Brown and Company, 1986.

Porter, Steven L. *Save Your Home: How to Protect Your Home & Property from Foreclosure.* Piccadilly Books, 1990.

Powell, Lynn S.(editor). *Foreclosure Management.* Mortgage Bankers, 1993.

Reilly, John W. *The Language of Real Estate,* 2nd ed. Real Estate Education Company, 1982.

Richards, Robert William. *The Dow Jones-Irwin Dictionary of Financial Planning.* Dow Jones-Irwin, 1986.

Santi, Albert. *The Mortgage Manual Q&A's on FHA, VA, and Conventional Mortgage Loans.* 4th ed. Probus Publishing Company, 1989.

Sheneman, Margaret. *California Foreclosure: Law & Practice.* Shepards-McGraw Publishers, 1991.

Sirkin, David A. *The Home Equity Sharing Manual,* John Wiley and Sons, 1994.

Steinmetz and Whitt, Phillip. *The Mortgage Kit, Third Edition.* Real Estate Education Co., 1994.

Sumichrast, Michael, and Shafeer, Ronald G. *The New Complete Book of Home Buying.* Dow Jones-Irwin, 1988.

Thomas, Ted; Powell, Judith, Editor. *Up for Grabs: Millions in Foreclosure Real Estate.* Top Mountain Publishers, 1993.

Thomas, Ted. *Big Money in Real Estate Foreclosures.* John Wiley and Sons, 1992.

Thomas, Ted. *Foreclosure Gold Mining, An Illustrated Guide: High Profit, Low Risk Real Estate for the 90's.* New Growth Financial Publishers, 1991.

Thomsett, Michael and Jean. *Getting Started in Real Estate Investing.* John Wiley and Sons.

Turk, Martin E. *The New-Home Buyer's Guide.* Groom Books, 1994.

Vila, Bob. *Bob Vila's Guide to Buying Your*

Dream House. Little, Brown and Company, 1990.

Vrabel, Joseph P. *Massachusetts Foreclosures.* Massachusetts CLE, 1990.

Warren, K.; Mayor, Ken-Editor. *Making It!: How to Avoid Becoming Homeless.* Lone Star Texas, 1990.

Watkins, A.M. *Manufactured Houses, Fifth Edition.* Real Estate Education Co., 1994.

Weisberg, Michael. *New Jersey Mortgage & Foreclosure Law.* Butterworth Legal Publishers, 1993.

Wiedemer, James T. *The Smart Money Guide to Bargain Homes: How to Find & Buy Foreclosures.* Dearborn Finan, 1994.

Wiedemer, John P. *Real Estate Investment,* 4th ed. Prentice Hall, 1989.

Yarnell, Michael A.; Cammack, Kent E.; Salerno, Thomas J.; Apker,
Burton M. *Ins & Outs of Foreclosures.* Arizona State Bar, 1990.

Yohannes, A.G. *Real Estate Finance.* Chicago: Probus Publishing Company, 1988.

MAGAZINES

The following magazines often have articles of special interest to home owners and future home buyers.

Farm Journal
Forbes
Home Magazine
HomeOwner Magazine
Metropolitan Home
Mother Earth News
Old-House Journal
Practical Homeowner
Real Estate Today
U.S. News & World Report

Glossary

Adjustable Rate Mortgage (ARM). A variable rate mortgage where the interest rate is adjusted periodically according to a specified index.

Adjusted Sale Price. The selling price of a home less allowable expenses (e.g. commissions, repairs). Used when determining the amount of gain or loss on the sale.

Alienation. The transfer of title to real property from one owner to another.

Amortization. The process of reducing mortgage debt through equal monthly payments.

Amortization Schedule. A schedule showing how each loan payment is divided between principal and interest.

Annual Percentage Rate (APR). A percentage rate which includes the cost of interest, loan fees, and points combined. Lenders must provide you with the APR, which you can use for comparing rates from different lenders.

Application fee. A non-refundable fee charged by the lender for processing a borrower's loan application.

Appraisal. A professional estimate of the value of a property as of a given date.

Appreciation. An increase in value of real estate over time.

As is. Refers to a property sold without guarantees of any kind. The buyer is solely responsible for the property, as long as no fraud has been committed by the seller.

Assessed Value. The value of a property for tax purposes as determined by the County Tax Collector.

Assumption of Mortgage. A buyer of property becomes responsible for repaying an existing mortgage. Fixed-rate mortgages are usually not assumable; VA, FHA, and adjustable-rate mortgages may be.

Balloon Note. A mortgage loan where the final payment is much larger than the preceding monthly payments. The final payment is known as the balloon payment.

Basis. The original purchase price of a property, adjusted to determine the capital gain or loss on the sale of real estate.

Beneficiary. The lender on a note or deed of trust.

Beneficiary's Statement. A written report from the lender stating the terms and conditions of the loan, such as amounts still owed, interest rate, monthly payments, and so on.

Bi-weekly mortgage. A mortgage where payments are made every two weeks, instead of once a month.

Binder. A preliminary agreement between a buyer and seller of real estate, secured by earnest money. If the buyer is unable to complete the purchase, the earnest money is lost, unless the binder says that it must be refunded.

Blanket Mortgage. In a cooperative, the mortgage on the building as a whole—as opposed to "share loans" that buyers must obtain to finance the purchase of their individual units.

Broker. A licensed agent who receives a commission for negotiating the sale or lease of property.

Buffer Zone. An area specified by local government that separates one land use from another.

Building Codes. A set of minimum building standards regulated by local government.

Building Line or Setback. The distance from the boundary of a property beyond which construction may not take place.

Buy-down. To pre-pay interest, which has the effect of temporarily reducing the interest rate on a mortgage loan.

Buyer's broker. A broker hired by the buyer to negotiate on the buyer's behalf. This is different from the usual arrangement, where the seller hires a broker and pays the broker's commission.

Call. The lender's right to demand immediate payment of the loan balance if the borrower violates the terms of the loan agreement.

Cap. A limit on the increase in monthly payments for an adjustable-rate mortgage. Also called Payment Cap.

Caveat Emptor. Let the buyer beware. The property is sold without guarantees.

Certificate of Eligibility. A certificate issued by the VA to set the maximum loan that the VA will guarantee.

Certificate of Title. A certificate issued by a title company or an attorney showing that the seller has clear title to the property offered for sale.

Closing. A meeting where the deed to a property is transferred from the seller to the buyer.

Closing Agent. The escrow agent who presides at the closing.

Closing Costs. The fees that must be paid to complete the transfer of ownership. The borrower is usually responsible for paying these fees, but the seller may contribute all or part of the costs.

Closing Statement. The final report of a sale by escrow, given to the buyer and the seller.

Collateral. Property used to secure a loan.

Commission. Money paid to a real estate broker upon completion of a real estate sale.

Commitment. The lender's notice to the borrower that the mortgage has been approved. The notice should explain the terms and conditions of the loan.

Common areas. In a condominium or cooperative, the property jointly owned by all unit owners.

Comparative Analysis. A method of appraising property that uses the selling prices of similar properties as the basis for arriving at a property's value.

Condition Precedent. A condition that must be met before title can be transferred.

Condition Subsequent. A clause which says that, if the owner fails to meet certain conditions, he or she may lose title to the property.

Conditional Sale Contract. A contract for the sale of property that gives conditions which must be fulfilled before delivery is made to the buyer.

Condo Fee (AKA Maintenance Fee). The monthly maintenance fee paid by condominium unit owners as their share of common area expenses.

Contingency. A condition or conditions specified in the loan or purchase contract, which must be met before the sale is final.

Conventional Loan. A loan that is not insured by the government.

Conventional Mortgage. Any mortgage that is not insured by HUD or guaranteed by the VA.

Convertible option. A provision in some adjustable-rate mortgages (ARMs) that allows the borrower to convert to a fixed rate under certain conditions.

Conveyance. A written document that transfers title from one owner to another. A deed, bill of sale, or an assignment may be used as conveyances.

Cooperative. A multi-unit property jointly owned by individual cooperative members, who have long-term leases on their units and own shares in a corporation that owns the building.

Counteroffer. An offer by the seller in response to a proposed offer by the buyer.

Credit check. A review of the borrower's payment record on loans, credit cards, and charge accounts.

Credit Life Insurance. Insurance that will repay the remaining loan balance to the bank upon the death of the borrower.

Credit report. A statement of the borrower's credit record, which the lender obtains prior to approving a loan.

Deed. A legal instrument which, when properly executed and delivered, conveys title to real property.

Deed Restrictions. Provisions placed in deeds by the owner to restrict future use of the property.

Default. Failure to make payments as agreed in a mortgage or deed of trust.

Deferral of Gain. A legal means of postponing taxes due from the sale of a house by buying a new house for the same amount, or more.

Deposit. The portion of the purchase price paid by the buyer when the sales agreement is signed, and typically held in escrow until the sale is complete.

Depreciation. A decline in the value of real estate over time.

Discount Points. Prepaid interest by a borrower which in effect reduces the interest rate on the loan.

Documentary Tax. A state tax on the sale of all real property. Also known as transfer tax.

Down payment. The portion of the purchase price, paid by the borrower in cash, which may not be borrowed from the mortgage lender.

Dual agency. The broker in a real estate transaction represents both the buyer and the seller. This is illegal unless agreed to by both parties.

Due-on-Sale Clause. A clause that says the entire unpaid balance of the loan is due upon the sale of the property.

Earnest Money. A "good faith" deposit given to the seller by a potential buyer to secure the sale. If the sale is completed, the earnest money is applied against the down payment. If not, the deposit may or may not be refunded, according to the terms of the sales contract or binder.

Easement. The legal and limited right to use or cross another person's land, e.g. a utility easement gives a utility company the right to run wires or lay pipes across a property.

Encroachment. Any obstruction, building, or part of a building that extends beyond a legal boundary into neighboring land.

Encumbrance. Anything that affects or limits good or clear title and diminishes the land's value, such as zoning ordinances, easement rights, claims, mortgages, liens, charges, pending legal action, and unpaid taxes.

Equity. The difference between the fair market value of a property and any encumbrances against it, such as total amount of unpaid mortgage balances and any other liens or debts against the property.

Equity line of credit. A loan secured by the equity in a property. This is a revolving line of credit where the borrower pays interest only on the amount of credit used. As the principal is repaid, it is available to be borrowed again.

Escheat. When the property of an owner who dies without known lawful heirs is given to the state.

Escrow. The submission of money (or documents) to a neutral third party who is bonded by law to carry out the provisions of a real estate agreement or contract.

Escrow Account. A separate account set up by a lender to hold funds paid as part of monthly mortgage payments. The purpose is to cover yearly costs for things like mortgage insurance premiums, property taxes, hazard insurance premiums, and special assessments.

Escrow Company. A firm that specializes in closing real estate transactions.

Exclusion of Gain. Under Federal tax law, a $125,000 one-time exclusion from the capital gains tax on the sale of homes by citizens aged 55 or older.

Exclusive agency. An agreement between a seller and a real estate broker, giving the broker the exclusive right to sell a property—but specifying that the broker does not get a commission if the owner sells the property on his or her own.

Exclusive Right to Sell. Similar to exclusive agency, except that the broker is entitled to a commission even if the owner finds the buyer on his or her own.

Fair Market Value. The estimated selling price of a property, usually determined by an appraisal.

Federal Home Loan Mortgage Corporation (Freddie Mac). Similar to Fannie Mae, an organization that provides money to lenders, who in turn make home loans to individual buyers.

Federal Housing Administration (FHA). A federal agency that insures home loans against default. FHA loans allow the borrower to make a lower down payment than conventional loans.

Federal National Mortgage Association (Fannie Mae). A government agency that buys mortgage loans from banks, thus enabling the banks to loan more money to home buyers.

Federal Tax Lien. A lien placed on property by the United States government to recover unpaid taxes.

Fee Simple. The highest form of ownership: complete and unrestricted title by a real estate owner to his or her property. Also known as fee absolute, fee simple absolute, or absolute.

First Mortgage (or First Deed of Trust). The primary lien against a property, which is paid first in the event of foreclosure or bankruptcy.

Fixed Rate Mortgage (FRM). A mortgage where the interest rate remains the same throughout the term of the loan.

Fixtures. Items attached to the property (e.g. plumbing, lighting) and sold with the property, unless specifically excluded.

Forced Sale. An involuntary sale of real property whereby the owner is forced by law to sell a property for whatever it will bring. Usually the sale is carried out by someone other than the owner: a trustee, sheriff, judge, or another official.

Foreclosure. A legal process where a lender takes back property owned by a borrower who has defaulted on a loan.

Full Disclosure. The obligation of a seller to reveal all facts that pertain to the sale of a property.

General Index. The county's record of all documents filed, organized alphabetically by names of parties involved.

General Warranty Deed. A deed that transfers title and guarantees that the title is free of all encumbrances (such as claims, judgments, or liens).

Good faith estimate. An estimate of closing costs, made by the lender within three days of the time an application for a loan is submitted by a borrower.

Graduated Payment Mortgage. A fixed-rate mortgage whose monthly payments increase, usually annually, over the term of the loan.

Grantee. The buyer or recipient.

Grantor. The seller or giver.

Hazard Insurance. A homeowners policy required by mortgage lenders to insure against damages caused by fire, windstorms, and other common hazards. Flood insurance is not usually part of a hazard insurance policy.

Home Equity Loan. A second mortgage borrowed against the equity in a home.

Home Equity Sales Contract. Purchase agreement between owner and buyer whereby the buyer purchases the equity value.

Home Inspection. A professional inspection to determine a home's overall condition and identify structural and/or mechanical problems.

HUD-1 Form. A statement detailing all the loan closing costs and itemizing all payments made by and due from both the buyer and the seller. Also known as the RESPA statement.

Impound Account. A bank account maintained by a borrower at the request of a lender to pay taxes and insurance on a property.

Improvement. Any modification that increases a property's value or useful life, or that adapts it to a new use.

Index Rate. A rate used by lenders to make periodic adjustments in adjustable-rate mortgages.

Inspection contingency. A clause in a purchase agreement that makes the sale contingent on the outcome of a structural and/or pest inspection.

Installment Contract. A contract where the seller finances the purchase and receives installment payments from the buyer.

Institutional Lender. Financial institutions whose loans are regulated by law, including banks, savings and loans, thrift and loans, insurance companies, credit unions, and commercial loan agencies.

Instrument. A legally binding written document.

Interest. An amount earned by a lender for the service of lending money.

Involuntary Lien. A lien placed against property without consent of the owner; i.e. for taxes or special assessments.

Joint and Several Note. A note signed by two or more parties in which they are jointly in and individually liable for the full amount of the note.

Joint Tenancy. Equal ownership by two or more persons in a property.

Judgment Lien. A lien placed against the property of a debtor by court order.

Junior Lien. A lien that does not have first claim on a property; e.g. judgments, taxes, second mortgages.

Lease. A contract that transfers possession and use of a property for a limited period under certain conditions.

Legal Description. A proper and formal description of a parcel of real estate that is recognized by law.

Leverage. To acquire property with borrowed money.

Lien. A legal claim against a property for money owed; it may be against a specific property or against all the property of the debtor.

Liquid Assets. Cash and assets that can be sold at near market value immediately for cash.

Listing. A real estate broker's description of properties available for sale.

Loan-to-Value Ratio (LTV). The percentage of a property's value that a lender will mortgage.

Loss Payee. The recipient of an insurance claim for a loss or damage.

Maintenance Fee. A fee paid monthly by condominium and cooperative owners.

Margin. An amount added to an index rate (usually 2 or 3 percent) to determine the borrower's interest rate.

Market Value. The price for which property can be sold when the seller and buyer are not under pressure to sell or buy quickly.

Marketable Title. A title that can be sold freely. A title that is free and clear of liens and other defects.

Mechanic's Lien. A lien placed on property by laborers and material suppliers for construction work.

Mortgage. To buy a piece of property using the property itself as security for a loan.

Mortgage Broker. Someone who finds mortgage lenders for interested borrowers.

Mortgage Insurance. An insurance policy required to protect the lender in case the borrower defaults on a loan.

Mortgage Insurance Premium (MIP). A payment made by the borrower to the lender to protect the lender against losses resulting from default. Required for FHA loans.

Mortgage Note. A written agreement to repay a loan, secured by a mortgage, which states the interest rate and manner in which the note shall be repaid.

Mortgagee. The lender on a mortgage.

Mortgagor. A borrower who wants a mortgage.

Multiple Listing Service (MLS). A network of real estate brokers. Property that is listed with one broker may also be shown by other brokers participating in the network.

Negative Amortization. When the interest on a note is not fully covered by the monthly payments, the balance of the principal increases instead of decreasing.

Net Worth. The difference between total assets and total liabilities.

No-documentation Loan. A type of loan that has fewer requirements than the standard loan approval process. Borrowers must usually make a relatively large down payment.

Notarize. To witness a signature on a document and to place a Notary Public's seal on that document.

Notary Public. A person authorized by the state to witness signatures.

Note. A legal agreement where the signer promises to pay a definite sum of money at a specified date or on demand. The note usually provides for interest, and may be secured by a deed of trust or a mortgage. Also known as a Promissory Note.

Notice of Default. A notice stating that the borrower under a mortgage or deed of trust has not made payments as agreed.

Notice of Trustee's Sale. The final notice required before a foreclosure auction. The notice must be recorded in the county recorder's office, advertised and posted. It states the time and location of the trustee's sale, and the legal description of the property to be sold.

Offer to Purchase. A formal document where a prospective buyer proposes to purchase a property for a certain amount and under certain terms and conditions. Acceptance of the offer creates a contract binding on both parties.

Open Listing. A listing agreement under which any broker may sell the property and receive a commission.

Open-End Mortgage. A mortgage with a provision that allows the owner to borrow additional money in the future without refinancing or additional charges.

Option. A provision in a contract that gives the buyer the right to buy or lease a property, specifying the price, time period and terms. An option provides the right to buy or sell, but is not a requirement to do so.

Origination fee. A fee charged by the lender for processing a borrower's loan application. The fee is calculated in points as a percentage of the loan, and is due at the closing.

Owner-occupied property. Property that will be occupied by the buyers, as opposed to investor-owned property. Some loans require that the property be occupied by the buyers.

Personal property. Any property that is not real estate.

Personal-use property. Real estate that is deemed for personal use, and therefore that can't be depreciated on income taxes.

Pest Inspection. Often included as a contingency in a Purchase and Sale agreement. A professional inspection for past or present pest damage.

PITI. Principal, interest, taxes, and insurance. The total monthly mortgage payment.

Planned Unit Development (PUD). A subdivision of individually owned lots and residences, with community ownership of common areas.

Plat. A drawing of a lot, subdivision, or community by a surveyor, which shows boundary lines, buildings, improvements, and easements.

Points. The fee mortgage lenders charge for processing a loan. Each point represents 1% of the mortgage amount. Points can be paid as a form of prepaid interest, to reduce the annual interest rate.

Pre-approval. To receive approval from the lender for a mortgage before the application is complete. Does not necessarily mean a formal commitment by the lender to make the loan. Not to be confused with pre-qualification.

Pre-qualification. An informal estimate made by the lender of the maximum mortgage a home buyer can borrow, based on the buyer's available income and existing debt.

Preliminary Title Report. An initial report from a title company on the present condition of title, made prior to issuing a title policy.

Prepayment Penalty. A fee that some lenders charge borrowers for repaying their loan early. FHA and VA loans do not have prepayment penalties.

Prime Rate. The rate charged to lenders by the Federal government, determined by the Federal Reserve. Often used as an index for adjustable rate mortgages.

Principal. The balance due on a loan, note, or debt, upon which interest is paid.

Private Mortgage Insurance (PMI). An insurance policy provided by private companies, rather than the FHA or VA, designed to protect the lender if the borrower defaults on the mortgage. Usually required for borrowers making less than a 20% down payment.

Property Line. The legal boundary of a piece of property.

Property Tax. A tax levied on real estate, based on the purchase price or the value of the property.

Purchase Agreement. A contract between the buyer and seller specifying the terms and conditions for a sale of real property. Also known as Purchase and Sale (P & S) agreement.

Purchase Money Encumbrance. A mortgage or deed of trust given by the buyer to the seller as all or part of the purchase price.

Purchase Money Mortgage. A mortgage financed by the seller in which the buyer receives title, and the property serves as collateral for the loan.

Qualifying. At a foreclosure auction, potential bidders must prove that they have enough money to purchase the property. Also, potential borrowers must satisfy certain requirements (qualify) for a loan.

Quitclaim Deed. A deed that transfers title or interest, but offers no warrantees regarding the quality of the title or interest.

REO (Real Estate Owned). Properties that are owned by lenders after foreclosure.

Rate cap. The maximum increase allowed in the rate over the term of an adjustable-rate mortgage.

Rate Lock. To secure ("lock in") the interest rate at the time the loan commitment is made, even if rates rise (or fall) between the commitment and the closing.

Real Estate Settlement Procedures Act (RESPA). An act of Congress designed to protect home buyers from high settlement costs. It requires full disclosure in advance of estimated settlement costs.

Realtor. A real estate broker who is a member of the National Association of Realtors (NAR).

Reconveyance. A written document that transfers title to real property from the trustee to the owner upon full payment of a deed of trust.

Recording. To legally file documents with the county so as they become public record. Also known as Constructive Notice.

Recording fees. The fees for filing documents to clear and transfer title.

Refinancing. The process of obtaining a new mortgage, typically at a lower rate, to pay off and replace the existing mortgage.

Rehabilitation. To restore of a property to satisfactory condition without drastically changing the plan, form or style of architecture.

Reinstatement Period. A period of three months following the recording of a notice of default. The owner may remedy the default by paying the balance owed to the lender.

Release of Mortgage. A document, like a reconveyance, issued by the lender that states that a loan has been paid in full.

Replacement period. The period allowed by the tax laws for buying another primary residence, in order to defer the gain realized on the sale of the former residence.

Repossession. A property which a lender owns after a foreclosure. The lender has "repossessed" the property upon which they loaned money.

Rescission. The mutual agreement by parties to a contract to void the contract.

Reserve fund. Money that is set aside by a condominium or cooperative association to finance large expenditures or necessary repairs.

Restraint of bidding. An agreement by two or more parties to limit bidding on a property being sold at a foreclosure auction. Such an agreement is illegal.

Restrictive Covenants. Private restrictions set in a deed which limit the use of real property. They binds all subsequent owners.

Rider. A clause added to an agreement specifying additional conditions or terms. Also known as an addendum.

Right of First Refusal. An owner's promise to allow an individual or entity to make the first offer when a property is put up for sale, or to match an offer submitted by another potential buyer.

Right of Survivorship. To automatically transfer interest in a property to the surviving owners upon the death of joint owner.

Sales Agent. An agent licensed to sell real estate under the supervision of a licensed broker.

Sales Agreement. A contract between a buyer and seller regarding the sale of a property. Also known as a purchase agreement.

Second Mortgage. An additional loan behind the first mortgage, also secured by the property. Usually has a higher interest rate and a shorter term that the first mortgage.

Secondary Financing. A term that refers to junior trust deeds or second mortgages.

Setback requirements. Local regulations which specify the distances required between homes, structures, and property boundaries, and between homes and streets.

Settlement. The real estate closing, where all funds are disbursed and a full accounting is made of the sale.

Shared Appreciation Mortgage. A loan that allows the lender to benefit from a portion of the property's appreciation.

Sole ownership. Possession by a single person or entity, as opposed to joint property ownership.

Special Assessments. A lien placed on real property for road construction, sidewalks, sewers, street lights, etc.

Special Warranty Deed. A deed that warrants the title against defects or claims. The seller promises to defend the title against any claims filed by or through the seller's heirs.

Survey. A map made by a licensed surveyor that shows a lot's legal boundaries, improvements, topography, and relationship to surrounding tracts of land.

Tenancy in Common. Undivided ownership of property by two or more persons, without right of survivorship. A deceased owner's share transfers to his or her heirs, rather than the other owner.

Term Loan. A loan where only the interest is paid until maturity, at which time the entire principal is due.

Title. A written document, usually a title insurance policy, that confirms rights of ownership.

Title Flaw. Any encumbrance on a title that hinders an owner's ability to transfer ownership.

Title Insurance. Insurance protection against loss of the property due to legal defects in title.

Title Search. A detailed examination of all recorded documents to ensure that the title is free of liens or other encumbrances, and that the seller has legal ownership.

Transfer Fees. The fees charged by some states and local governments whenever real property is sold.

"Truth-in-Lending" disclosure statement. Required by federal law, this is a written statement made to the borrower containing detailed information about the terms and costs of the loan.

Underwriting guidelines. The rules and standards used by lenders to determine a borrower's eligibility for a loan.

VA loans. Mortgages guaranteed by the Veterans Administration and available to eligible veterans, their spouses and dependents.

Variable Rate Mortgage. Any mortgage whose interest rate rises or falls according to a specified interest rate, for example, the prime rate.

Voluntary Lien. Any lien placed on property by the voluntary act of the owner—for example, a mortgage.

Waiver. A written document where a party voluntarily surrenders a claim, benefit, or right.

Warrantee. A legally binding written or implied guarantee that property (including mechanical systems or appliances) is in good condition and will perform as promised.

Wrap-Around Mortgage. A mortgage that includes the first mortgage and possibly any second mortgages—without refinancing the first mortgage at substantially higher current rates.

Zoning Ordinances. Local laws that establish building codes and other restrictions for real estate use in a given area.

Index

NOTES

NOTES